Rebuilding Together

The 12-Week Therapy Workbook Every Couple Must Have for Building a Stronger Relationship, Improving Communication, and Creating a More Meaningful Connection

Rachel Morgan

Rachel Morgan © Copyright 2023 - All rights reserved.

The content contained within this book may not be reproduced, duplicated or transmitted without direct written permission from the author or the publisher.

Under no circumstances will any blame or legal responsibility be held against the publisher, or author, for any damages, reparation, or monetary loss due to the information contained within this book. Either directly or indirectly.

Legal Notice:

This book is copyright protected. This book is only for personal use. You cannot amend, distribute, sell, use, quote or paraphrase any part, or the content within this book, without the consent of the author or publisher.

Disclaimer Notice:

Please note the information contained within this document is for educational and entertainment purposes only. All effort has been executed to present accurate, up to date, and reliable, complete information. No warranties of any kind are declared or implied. Readers acknowledge that the author is not engaging in the rendering of legal, financial, medical or professional advice. The content within this book has been derived from various sources. Please consult a licensed professional before attempting any techniques outlined in this book.

By reading this document, the reader agrees that under no circumstances is the author responsible for any losses, direct or indirect, which are incurred as a result of the use of information contained within this document, including, but not limited to, — errors, omissions, or inaccuracies.

TABLE OF CONTENTS

Introduction — 11

Chapter 1. Who is this book for? — 12

Chapter 2. How to use this book and what benefits you will find in reading it — 19

Chapter 3. 12-week program for couples — 22

Week 1. How to improve couple communication — 24

    Tip 1: be sincere and avoid having secrets — 26

    Tip 2: learn to regulate your tone of voice — 27

    Tip 3: express your appreciation to your partner — 28

    Tip 4: learn to communicate to understand each other better and learn to forgive yourself — 28

    Tip 5: try to accept your vulnerability, without fear of showing it to your partner — 29

    Tip 6: improve couple communication also using physical language — 29

    Tip 7: stop taking everything for granted and learn to be direct — 30

    Tip 8: learn the art of silence — 31

    Tip 9: learn to listen actively — 31

    Tip 10: act as if you are a team and not a single player — 32

Week 2. How to handle money problems — 33

    Tip 1: be honest about your financial situation — 34

Tip 2: clarify immediately what lifestyle you intend to lead — 34

Tip 3: even if you want to maintain your individual autonomy, try to achieve common goals. — 35

Tip 4: define which costs are essential, and which are not — 36

Tip 5: identify your long-term and short-term goals — 36

Tip 6: split the expenses — 37

Tip 7: invest your savings — 37

Tip 8: use the same approach when handling money — 38

Tip 9: monitor all purchases — 38

Tip 10: use technology to monitor your finances — 38

Week 3. How to improve intimacy as a couple — 40

Tip 1: talk about the decline in desire — 41

Tip 2: take time just for you — 42

Tip 3: change your approach — 43

Tip 4: communicate with your partner and talk about your fears and desires — 43

Tip 5: take care of your relationship by fighting boredom and monotony — 44

Tip 6: make your partner feel special — 45

Tip 7: write a wish list — 45

Tip 8: always celebrate your moments of connection — 46

Tip 9: increase physical contact — 47

Tip 10: try to see the positive sides of your partner every day — 48

Week 4. How to handle the senseless fights of the couple — 49

Tip 1: start taking personal responsibility and apologizing if necessary. — 50

Tip 2: stop and start thinking about what you are doing or saying — 51

Tip 3: don't blame each other — 52

Tip 4: let go of the conflict even when you think reason is on your side — 52

Tip 5: learn to listen and avoid attacking — 53

Tip 6: leave the past behind — 53

Tip 7: give appropriate time and space for the argument — 54

Tip 8: include the possibility of a time-out during your discussions — 54

Tip 9: try to understand each other's feelings — 55

Tip 10: be careful how and when you express your opinions — 56

Week 5. How to manage work and career — 57

Tip 1: avoid having lunch together — 58

Tip 2: treat yourself to a day of relaxation without talking about work — 58

Tip 3: maintain decorum and professionalism — 58

Tip 4: never mix private life and career together — 59

Tip 5: try not to compete — 59

Tip 6: learn to manage stress levels due to your work situation — 59

Tip 7: learn to balance work and private life — 60

Tip 8: don't hide your worries and work problems — 60

Tip 9: trust each other ... 61

Tip 10: don't change your plans ... 61

Week 6. How to manage social relationships ... 63

Tip 1: take care of your individuality ... 64

Tip 2: go gradually ... 65

Tip 3: make your friends accept your partner ... 65

Tip 4: avoid your relationship becoming all-encompassing ... 66

Tip 5: try to find the right balance ... 67

Tip 6: try to make friends and social relationships as a priority as such in your relationship as a couple. ... 68

Tip 7: give your attention to the needs of others ... 68

Tip 8: try to make your partner understand the benefits of social relationships ... 69

Tip 9: involve your partner in hanging out with groups of other friends more often. ... 69

Tip 10: try to be available and always respond to messages, calls or emails from your relatives and friends. ... 70

Week 7. How to manage extra-work activities as a couple ... 71

Tip 1: try something new ... 72

Tip 2: plan a relaxed day after work for just the two of you. ... 72

Tip 3: an infallible classic, a romantic dinner at home ... 73

Tip 4: host a game night ... 74

Tip 5: organize an evening dedicated only to you and to music	74
Tip 6: do not plan anything but leave everything to improvisation	74
Tip 7: organize an evening dedicated to your passions	75
Tip 8: dedicate a romantic evening to dinner in a starred restaurant.	75
Tip 9: throw a party to celebrate everything you've been through together	76
Tip 10: choose a new interest to do together	76

Week 8. How to manage free time as a couple — 77

Tip 1: take courses in creative writing	79
Tip 2: go dancing together	79
Tip 3: go camping	79
Tip 4: take cooking lessons	80
Tip 5: dedicate yourself to hiking	80
Tip 6: take holidays and trips as a couple	80
Tip 7: do DIY	81
Tip 8: read together	81
Tip 9: decorate a room together	82
Tip 10: Exercise together	82

Week 9. How to improve romance as a couple — 83

Tip 1: awaken romance by starting the day with a romantic gesture	84
Tip 2: awaken romance with unexpected gifts	85

Tip 3: keep sexuality alive — 85

Tip 4: make a fixed appointment — 86

Tip 5: only fall asleep after a goodnight kiss — 86

Tip 6: visit the place where you first met — 87

Tip 7: write a letter — 87

Tip 8: plan a romantic date — 87

Tip 9: give to your partner something made by you — 88

Tip 10: remind yourself every day why your partner is the love of your life — 88

Week 10. How to best manage cohabitation — 90

Tip 1: carefully choose the house where you are going to live together — 91

Tip 2: establish early on how to manage expenses — 92

Tip 3: establish early on how to handle cleaning and household chores — 92

Tip 4: face the difficulties of living together by communicating — 93

Tip 5: create a couple space — 94

Tip 6: respect each other's habits — 94

Tip 7: carve out some time just for yourself — 95

Tip 8: avoid outside interference in your relationship decisions — 96

Tip 9: Don't let your relationship become monotonous — 96

Tip 10: Try to resolve issues by making compromises — 97

Week 11. How to manage the decision-making aspects of the couple
98

Tip 1: improve your ability to meet each other … 99

Tip 2: try to be more empathetic towards each other … 100

Tip 3: always talk to make the right decision … 101

Tip 4: always try to remain a united couple, even when deciding … 101

Tip 5: avoid perpetual indecision … 102

Tip 6: always consider risk management … 102

Tip 8: never make important decisions for the other too … 103

Tip 9: try to find a new balance … 103

Tip 10: always try to reach the right compromise … 103

Week 12. How to improve mutual trust … 105

Tip 1: learn to be together … 106

Tip 2: try to always be there, especially in difficult times … 107

Tip 3: Express your thoughts and feelings freely … 107

Tip 4: Always try to be honest … 108

Tip 5: Always prefer to be clear and transparent … 108

Tip 6: never judge the other … 109

Tip 7: give each other the space you need … 110

Tip 8: never take the other for granted … 110

Tip 9: give importance to the little things … 110

Tip 10: keep your commitments ... 111

Conclusion ... 112

Introduction

In this guide you will find everything you need to know about couples therapy, about what are the benefits of tackling couple problems together and managing the various situations step by step.

You will be offered a 12-week therapy program, where you will find which situations to improve every week, with 10 practical tips to better manage every aspect of your relationship that will be taken into consideration.

The purpose of the guide will therefore be to show you how adequate couples therapy can be of considerable help to couples in dealing with moments of crisis. Understanding how to deal with relationship problems will not only help you get out of unpleasant situations, but at the same time it will make your relationship deeper and more grounded.

In a stable and lasting couple, there are many situations and many problems that one must go through. Positively overcoming these situations will profoundly change both the two partners and their relationship.

These changes, which don't always go in the same direction, can push the couple into a deep crisis. In this guide, therefore, all the situations that can give rise to these crises will be addressed, to save but also safeguard one's relationship. So, as you can well understand, this guide will not only be useful for couples with serious relationship problems, therefore already in a critical phase, but it can also be desirable for those couples with a good relationship, to improve communication, prevent future conflicts, maintain a more harmonious relationship, as well as to strengthen their bond and get to know each other better.

Chapter 1. Who is this book for?

The couple's relationship is not static, but dynamic, in the sense that it tends to change and evolve. From the first meeting, through the formation of the actual couple, the feelings that bind the two individuals are constantly changing. Initially, the physical attraction prevails which can quickly evolve into the condition of falling in love. With the deepening of mutual knowledge, the relationship between the two partners becomes more stable and solid, but the overwhelming emotions of the beginning become more and more nuanced. This is the moment in which space is left for a more realistic and objective evaluation of the partner, we begin to see their defects and what distances us from the other. The disappointment of the expectations, placed up to that moment on the partner, can give rise to doubts about the possibility of continuing a relationship that is different from what we had imagined.

This guide, therefore, addresses the couple: attention is focused on the relationship and the changes that can be made to it; the main purpose is to overcome the crisis and recover an understanding so that the relationship can be lived in a new, more constructive, and satisfying way.

But what are the signs that the couple works disharmonically? What do we observe in a couple who needs couples therapy?

John Gottman, the famous American psychologist considered an authority in the field of couple psychotherapy, has identified four behaviors that represent the signs of a probable breakup of the couple.

Criticize. Gottman observed that couples that are en route to breaking up are characterized by the fact that the partners express criticism of each other more than they express appreciation.

Most criticisms that partner exchange concern differences in preferences and tastes. In practice, partners tend to criticize each other for being different and this will never lead to anything good, if only because the differences will remain anyway, and it will certainly not be a criticism that will change the other. In short, most of the criticisms exchanged by partners are sterile. They do not produce positive changes, approaches, and mutual understanding.

In successful couples, on the other hand, the partners have learned to accept and even value differences. They have realized that the other can't be a copy of themselves.

Typically, at the beginning of the relationship, i.e., in the Romance Phase, the differences between the partners are not understood or minimized. But then, when the idyll comes to an end, because sooner or later the idyll does end, the same differences are experienced, first with nervousness, then with resentment, and, sometimes, with anger and increasingly frequent quarrels.

The problem is not in arguing. All couples do. The problem isn't even getting angry. This also happens in all couples and healthy people. The problem is not even in the criticisms related to specific behaviors. It is like human relationships not to agree on individual behaviors, to criticize them and ask to behave differently.

The problem lies in the criticisms which, perhaps starting as a pretext from specific behaviors, end up affecting the other person in their personality in their true essence. That is, the problem lies in criticizing the other person for who they are, not for what they do.

Despise. Being in a relationship is not always a happy and romantic experience. Sometimes even very intense negative emotions of fear, anger, and even hatred are experienced.

Even if the adult and rational part of us tells us that love as a couple can never be unconditional, sometimes our emotions go in another direction, and we feel disappointed and angry because we don't feel loved as we would like.

This is normal and happens to all couples. However, sometimes partners react to these intense negative emotions with strong reactions of contempt, insulting the other or attacking him to reduce his sense of self-worth. We try, in practice, to humiliate the other, even if we do it unconsciously.

In couples headed for a breakup, the tendency to react with contempt and intense hostility is the norm. On the contrary, harmonious couples tend to only rarely or never fall into contempt reactions: they usually have communication that tends to support and value the other.

Contempt manifests itself verbally and non-verbally in a tone of voice, gaze, posture, and gestures. Sarcasm, cynicism, eye-rolling, name calling are all manifestations of contempt. Contempt communicates that you feel disgusted with the other person. And, of course, it becomes impossible to clear up a disagreement when one partner becomes the object of the other's disgust. Or even worse when both partners despise each other.

You don't get to despise yourself in one day. Couples tend to put aside grievances that stem from unresolved situations, perhaps for years. The set-aside resentment gradually becomes more intense and begins to manifest itself in the form of contempt, which gradually creeps into relational life and becomes an increasingly present and tolerated attitude. Contempt is a very powerful poison that, sooner or later, will undermine the very foundations of the relationship.

Despise. Being in a relationship is not always a happy and romantic experience. Sometimes even very intense negative emotions of fear, anger, and even hatred are experienced.

Even if the adult and rational part of us tells us that love as a couple can never be unconditional, sometimes our emotions go in another direction, and we feel disappointed and angry because we don't feel loved as we would like.

This is normal and happens to all couples. However, sometimes partners react to these intense negative emotions with strong reactions of contempt, insulting the other, or attacking him to reduce his sense of self-worth. We try, in practice, to humiliate the other, even if we do it unconsciously.

In couples headed for a breakup, the tendency to react with contempt and intense hostility is the norm. On the contrary, harmonious couples tend to only rarely or never fall into contempt reactions: they usually have communication that tends to support and value the other.

Contempt manifests itself verbally and non-verbally in a tone of voice, gaze, posture, and gestures. Sarcasm, cynicism, eye-rolling, name calling are all manifestations of contempt. Contempt communicates that you feel disgusted with the other person. And, of course, it becomes impossible to clear up a disagreement when one partner becomes the object of the other's disgust. Or even worse when both partners despise each other.

You don't get to despise yourself in one day. Couples tend to put aside grievances that stem from unresolved situations, perhaps for years. The set-aside resentment gradually becomes more intense and begins to manifest itself in the form of contempt, which gradually creeps into relational life and becomes an increasingly present and tolerated attitude. Contempt is a very powerful poison that, sooner or later, will undermine the very foundations of the relationship.

Be on the defensive. You get defensive when you feel criticized and despised and, consequently, you seek justifications for your mistakes or try to prove to others that you don't deserve the treatment you suffered.

Marriages are most likely to end and are characterized by a highly defensive attitude. In these couples, the partners spend a lot of time justifying themselves and trying to prove that each other's criticisms are unjustified.

Unfortunately, research has shown that this self-justifying attitude very rarely has the intended effect of changing another person's mind. What happens is that each partner becomes an island, stops listening to the other, and focuses only on their own justifications and point of view.

The emotional consequences of being defensive are that each partner will feel misunderstood and ultimately more alone.

Stonewalling. Stonewalling means withdrawing into oneself and cutting off all communication with the other. It usually happens that one partner tries to talk and the other stops communicating, no longer providing signals of wanting to understand or want to listen. In short, one partner communicates and the other ignores it. This attitude is more common among men than among women.

Often stonewalling is the attitude that a partner takes when he feels helpless and exasperated after a long period of quarrels marked by criticism, contempt, and defensive attitudes.

Some may feel that ignoring their partner is a way to reduce conflict and perhaps, over time, find peace. The absence of a response is like depriving the other of oxygen. In fact, research has shown that the absence of an answer stimulates in the other a sense of danger greater than even an attack or direct criticism.

Thus, when one partner ignores the other, it is possible that the second can come to feel that he does not exist, that he is not worthy, and that he is not lovable. This is because the emotional brain interprets being ignored as a sign of danger. In certain partners who have had a life history characterized by absent or neglectful parents, being ignored by one's partner can induce very intense fear responses. And equally intense anger.

As couple therapists know, it is easier to restore harmony between two partners who often argue than between two partners who have cut off their emotional communication. And clearly, the longer this interruption has taken place, the more difficult it is for the couple to heal.

It goes without saying that if you want to build a healthy and satisfying couple, these four behaviors must be stopped, or at least limited, at all costs. If you recognize that the destructive behaviors described above are part of your relationship as a couple, you may want to change that.

But how to discriminate when you need help from a couple of therapists?

The frequency with which the four dysfunctional behaviors occur must be considered. If criticism, contempt, defensive attitudes, and obstructionism are occasional, it is a sign that the partners have within themselves the resources to cope with a couple of problems and that sometimes they "slip" into destructive behavior only to later realize it (in explicitly or implicitly) and choose to do something different. If, on the other hand, they are present most of the time and the partners cannot find other more constructive ways of being together, then we need to take note of the stalemate in which the couple finds themselves.

In the event of a deadlock, it is necessary to intervene immediately. Couple problems don't resolve themselves, partners have to do something to change the situation. They must raise the issue and address it. They must change themselves to some extent. There is what doctors call spontaneous remission. This of course can be done in many different ways, there is not only the path of couple therapy from a psychotherapist. And it is for this reason that this guide was born, to help you deal with the moments of crisis and tension that may arise in your couple and resolve everything in a positive way.

Chapter 2. How to use this book and what benefits you will find in reading it

This guide has been designed to help you solve relationship problems by bringing both partners' relationships to a more normal and healthy level. Couple therapy developed in this guide demonstrates its relevance when it allows you to overcome a moment of crisis or difficulty in a relationship.

Through this therapeutic path, couples in crisis can find balance and significantly improve their relationship.

The objectives of this guide always depend on the type and extent of the problem. However, the following primary objectives will be covered in this guide:

Good communication and openness to dialogue in the relationship. Indeed, expressing feelings is very important to avoid insecurities, depression, or low self-esteem. More often than not, in fact, the root of couple conflicts lies in a lack of adequate and effective communication between the two parties.

Improving the relationship with small gestures: even just saying the word I love you is essential to make your partner feel desired and sure of your feelings.

Thanks to this guide you will find the following benefits within your relationship:

- Live a peaceful and fulfilling life as a couple
- Learn to manage difficult situations, such as tensions, worries, and loss of inner balance
- Overcome and manage moments of crisis, such as betrayal, monotony, loss of sexual attraction, or a lack of common interests
- Dialogue and communicate effectively by learning to recognize your partner's language
- Learn to understand your expectations, that is, to understand when these are excessive or unattainable, trying to be sincere and express your deepest needs without any fear.

With this guide, you will be able to better understand yourself and your partner. In fact, I will help both partners to express their feelings, their fears, their most intimate secrets, their needs, values, and beliefs.

Furthermore, thanks to this guide you will learn to communicate effectively between you, to ask your partner for what you really want without having to chase or accuse your partner of lack of interest in you.

However, one must not make the mistake of thinking that the aim is to force two people who no longer want to have anything to do with each other to get back together: the goal to be achieved, however, must be to try to verify the existence of a residual space that favors a new interaction and offers further opportunities for communication.

The primary purpose of this guide is instead to learn to listen to the needs of others and to take different points of view than your own. In addition, one could acquire a higher awareness of how attitudes, behaviors and mental patterns are able to influence emotions. The couple, therefore, is put in a position to be able to find different ways of communicating and to change their expectations and beliefs, so that the most irrational, the most counterproductive and the most destructive ones can be set aside.

In summary, the great benefit of the couple therapy presented in this guide consists in making available communication methods of which the partners are not aware: methods that allow resolving potential conflicts, but also to find a meeting point following treason or at any moment of difficulty. It is said that partners do not always have the magic wand that allows them to read each other's minds: over the years, in fact, communication skills can age, and perhaps become rusty. Thanks to the therapy shown in this book, it will be ensured that the contact between the two components of a couple rediscovers the authenticity and naturalness of the past, both from the point of view of physical understanding and from the point of view of emotional feeling. intellectual and sentimental, to create a stable and functional relationship.

Chapter 3. 12-week program for couples

Life in a couple of relationships is not always easy: it is not uncommon for problems to arise, situations of imbalance, and difficulties in communication which can lead to a difficult crisis to manage. In these and many other cases, couple therapy can help embark on a path of mutual improvement in the relationship between the two individuals of the couple.

In this guide, you will find a 12-week journey for couples to learn how to get in touch with their partner, resolve problems and discussions in a healthy way, how to be able to love each other more deeply and be able to communicate in a healthy and effective way.

The goal of this 12-week program is to build a new couple story, seeking different meanings in mutual events and behaviors and reconciling the individuality of each partner with belonging to the same couple dimension. Furthermore, the goal is both to restore balance and serenity in the couple and to lead the couple to make their life choices in a conscious way.

This path turns out to be an excellent tool of help when only one, or both partners, experience a lasting malaise. It is especially useful for couples under the check of repetitive dynamics that fuel misunderstandings and creates a vicious circle of frustration, leading to a decline in desire.

Thanks to this 12-week journey, you will therefore find how to overcome some daily problems that create dissatisfaction, recover understanding, rebuild trust and get closer to intimacy, experience the relationship in a more constructive and satisfying way.

Even the most functional couples can benefit from this path. Positive experiences suggest this type of therapy also proves useful for healthy partners who feel the desire to improve internal communication, strengthen the bond and better cope with changes and stressful events.

Week 1. How to improve couple communication

Often, when we are in an established relationship, we confuse good communication with just having a conversation. After all, having a conversation with your partner is necessary, but it's not the only way to demonstrate your feelings and ensure the smooth functioning of the relationship.

One of the reasons why communication breaks down and a relationship fails is that over time, anger or prejudice develops toward the partner. In this case, prejudice means that our partner has an idea of us (and we of him) that can be so deeply rooted that, even if we evolve, change, and grow, he always continues to see us through that idea. And we do the same with him. So often we believe we already know what our partner wants to tell us, his arguments, his reactions, and considerations about something and, in this way, we interrupt communication with our partner forever.

To lay solid foundations and be a successful couple, it is essential, to be honest with each other, be respectful towards each other, accept mistakes and improve communication as a couple.

Improving couple communication will certainly facilitate the relationship between the partners and the understanding between them.

Communicating means transmitting, and sharing information with an interlocutor; communication is always characterized by someone who sends a message, by the content of this message, which will be disseminated in a particular way and by the effect that the message has on the recipient.

We understand well how the complexity of the couple is added to the complexity of communication. For a couple to be in balance it is important that the members of each couple are every human being inserted in a relationship, must first of all be sufficiently in harmony with himself, maintain his own identity and then interact with the other by finding common sharing spaces. From all this we understand how complicated it is to live a couple relationship in a healthy way and above all how difficult and complicated communication as a couple is often.

Communication is one of the most important elements in a couple; whether it goes well or badly, completing it satisfies both members of a relationship. Good communication, therefore, is a guarantee of a satisfactory relationship with a future, while poor communication practically ensures the not very distant failure of a couple.

In this sense, both the content of the communication and the way of transmitting it and the context in which it takes place are very important. It is not the same to say "stupid" with an angry face and shout as with a seductive expression and whispers.

If we want to improve communication in the couple, we must also pay attention to:

- Do not frequently interrupt the other while he or she is talking, perhaps trying to give advice if not requested

- Rambling and constantly changing the subject while the other is trying to tell us about something important to him or her
- Listen in a disinterested and apathetic way when the other is talking to us.

Anticipation, as well as assuming and hypothesizing what the partner thinks or wants, is one of the most common mistakes in communication.

Catastrophism is an element that abruptly ends communication. Don't wait to hit rock bottom, better act before things gets really tough. A side effect that worsens the picture is the use of physical force, which reinforces the catastrophic messages.

Absolutism and extremism, which have to do with the inability to accept points of view different from one's own, lead to a lack of self-control and the difficulty of calmly observing the situation. They often involve enforcing certain behaviors or displaying exaggerated emotional responses.

Dogmatism, morality, and excessive vagueness are enemies of good communication.

Complaining, pointing out, blaming, reproaching, and judging the partner are the main causes of communication failure.

After talking about what couple communication is and what mistakes to avoid, let's see in practice what are the 10 best tips to improve it.

Tip 1: be sincere and avoid having secrets

In any relationship, there can be a secret, with the idea of sharing it later. Lots of little secrets, like a surprise gift or delicate topics that you still don't feel like revealing.

It is comprehensible. In some cases, these surprises can be extra for the relationship. However, to improve communication as a couple you must avoid secrets related to your past.

If something has hurt you or if you have a situation that you find difficult to talk about, take some time, but remember that sooner or later you will have to face it. What matters is that your partner knows that there is a topic that is troubling you and that you are not yet able to talk about.

You may find yourself having to answer some questions and you must, therefore, be prepared because they are normal. You think your partner might be worried about what is happening to you and how it affects your life.

Tip 2: learn to regulate your tone of voice

Many arguments lead to big fights, not about what is said but about the tone in which it is said. To improve communication as a couple and in any other relationship, it is important that we understand how we are talking to our partner.

Raising the tone of the voice is useless in almost all cases. You probably do it so that your opinions are heard, but it could also have the opposite effect, making the other person more and more annoyed. Maybe because you don't realize that when you raise the volume of your voice, you're somehow trying to belittle what your partner is saying.

Tip 3: express your appreciation to your partner

Good couple communication also consists in staying in tune not only in difficult moments but above all during positive situations. Couples who communicate correctly and positively also do so to express their love and mutual respect. The way to show appreciation can be done through sweet and loving words or by complimenting the partner on the results achieved.

These thoughtful words and appreciation can be very helpful on busy days, or times when there are many distractions.

A practical example to improve this aspect of communication could be to bring flowers or a small thought to your partner when he has had a bad day and just needs to be consoled and comforted.

Another fundamental element to increase this aspect of communication skills is to know how to say thank you. There are words that have a hidden power and when we use them, without realizing it, they can often give, both to those who say them and to those who receive them, more than we think. One of these is the word thank you. When your partner does something kind and nice, even if you are an established couple, never forget to say thank you.

Tip 4: learn to communicate to understand each other better and learn to forgive yourself

Forgiving your partner and accepting personal mistakes when a negative or complex situation has occurred helps improve communication as a couple.

It sounds easy, but it's not, because being willing to forgive a partner's mistake also means being willing to improve yourself. We must clarify the errors of both, in an objective way. When you have found common ground on the origin of the shortcomings, talk to find alternatives that allow you to avoid the same situation from happening again in the future.

Tip 5: try to accept your vulnerability, without fear of showing it to your partner

One of the ways to improve communication as a couple is to show yourself a little vulnerable to the other person. We are referring to giving yourself the opportunity to express those emotions that you usually try to hide.

No one likes to do this, some think that letting others see their fears, frustrations, and traumas makes them weak and easy prey.

However, if you can't be vulnerable with your partner and count on their support, who could you do it with? If you are with someone you love and want to share the best of your life with, you must also allow them to see your dark sides.

Tip 6: improve couple communication also using physical language

If your partner struggles to express her emotions, words may not be enough. Learn to break moments of tension even with a hug, to help him feel taken by the hand, listened to, and understood.

Sometimes, improving communication as a couple means knowing how to listen and knowing how to stay silent so that the other can let off steam. Even if you can't do something specific to help him, this small step is very helpful and will help your partner slowly open to dialogue as well.

Physical contact will allow you to communicate without the need to speak. Also knowing the non-verbal language of the other your relationship will rise to a much deeper level.

Tip 7: stop taking everything for granted and learn to be direct

Another way to improve communication as a couple is to stop making assumptions about whether your partner will do or say a certain thing. When we take something for granted, we label the other person, who may lose any interest in surprising us.

Moreover, in most cases, we make assumptions based on our expectations. If you make this mistake, you could be sabotaging your partner, your relationship, and yourself. Even if he repeats a certain behavior, give yourself a chance to be open to other responses.

Instead, try to always be direct when communicating with your partner. Write this phrase somewhere to always keep it in mind and remember what it means. Many times, one cannot speak clearly. The irony and sarcasm are used or the other is instigated with phrases like you know very well what is there.

Are you really sure your partner can read your thoughts? As we have already said before, you should never take anything for granted. Being direct and honest is essential to improve communication as a couple. It means avoiding conflicts and resolving them without wasting time unnecessarily. If you don't like something, look for the simplest and clearest way to say it.

When something unpleasant happens, try over the next 4 days to analyze how you feel when you are silent or not direct with your partner. You probably feel ashamed or perhaps you will begin to doubt that the other can understand you simply by observing you Analyzing all the aspects and emotions that led you to act in a certain way will only improve your communication as a couple.

Tip 8: learn the art of silence

First of all, to create a channel of understanding and respect, it is essential to leave room for silence, with communication that is reduced in terms of the number of words, but high in quality. Words can be few but incisive: express your feelings and enrich the dialogue with non-verbal codes, such as affectionate gestures or looks, evocative silences, and a calm tone. Take silent breaks whenever you feel that an emotion is overwhelming your mind and return to giving verbal form to your feelings when you have clarified what you are feeling. In particular, if you are angry, do not argue persistently.

Tip 9: learn to listen actively

Active listening is a great communication tool. Knowing how to listen without interrupting your partner, observing her body language and in the meantime managing your verbal and non-verbal communication are key elements. One of the techniques is a reformulation, which consists in paraphrasing the message to understand if it has been received appropriately, as well as verifying that what has been captured is exactly what the partner wanted to communicate; this allows you to go deeper and get to know each other better. Other techniques that strengthen listening are summarizing, underlining some concepts, or verbalizing the emotional state of the other.

Tip 10: act as if you are a team and not a single player

The last tip to improve communication as a couple concerns the ability to see the relationship as a team effort. When there are conflicts, there is sometimes a tendency to blame the other party. This makes the couple lose their perspective: they play on the same team; they are not rivals. Always keep this concept in mind and tackle problems together, collaborating.

Week 2. How to handle money problems

Problems related to money, or its management is often the subject of discussions and quarrels within many emotional relationships. The management of money in the couple is therefore an aspect that should not be underestimated since many people have a perception of money that is very different from that of others.

The perception we have of money and how to manage it is learned and internalized by the family history of each of us. The economic models, linked to spending and savings, are in fact behavioral aspects that are handed down from parents to their children. This leads us to very different and unexpected situations once we decide to share our life with another person.

When you start a relationship, you pay more attention to the aspects in which you are in tune: hobbies, values, future plans, same experiences. In this phase of the relationship, almost no one takes into consideration the economic aspect or the economic availability of the other.

Talking about the economic aspect of the person with whom we have decided to share life is neither superficiality nor a violation of the privacy of the other. The reason for doing so is only to understand if it is possible to be able to support a common project not only on an emotional level but also on an economic level.

When it comes to money within a couple, communication is of paramount importance. Managing finances together with another person requires a lot of communication and trust. Even the most compatible couples can have very different attitudes about money, so it's important to approach finances openly and honestly.

Problems related to money in the relationship usually cause frequent quarrels and in many cases the breakup of the relationship. Let's see what tips can be useful in these cases.

Tip 1: be honest about your financial situation

When you're in a relationship and considering moving in together, be honest about your financial situation and be clear about your salary. It is not a matter of indiscretion or lack of trust in the other, but it serves to know if both partners are able to face the costs of running the house or the expenses necessary to face the purchase of the house or to pay all the extra expenses that may arise once you start living together.

Having a relationship under the same roof also implies facing expenses together and for this reason it is a priority to clarify the real economic situation of both.

Tip 2: clarify immediately what lifestyle you intend to lead

A fundamental aspect of managing money in the couple is clarifying which lifestyle you want to lead. If the goal is to save to achieve a specific goal, the daily life of the relationship will be marked by saving to achieve the goal.

Both partners must agree on these goals and meet them equally. Otherwise, insurmountable conflicts will undoubtedly arise within the couple.

Tip 3: even if you want to maintain your individual autonomy, try to achieve common goals.

Sometimes financial abuse occurs in an emotional relationship. This means that only one of the two controls the couple's expenses. Furthermore, in some cases, the other person does not even have the possibility to access the account. So that the relationship is happy and fulfilling, both must have full autonomy of their own accounts. There cannot be a single person who holds the account and who decides on two. We must have full mutual trust knowing that we have a common goal; two responsible people engaged in household chores.

Sharing goals to choose and focus on those considered fundamental and priority is the best gift you can give to love, improving life as a couple and skyrocketing the quality of life for both.

In order not to give up your financial independence, sharing is essential. When the situation is analyzed in an accurate and shared way, in fact, it becomes natural and easier to know and monitor the economic condition of the couple, evaluating the progress towards the achievement of a common goal and, consequently, keeping in mind the margin disposition. And this is not a trivial matter, given that knowing the context in which one is living helps in many cases to indulge in a few more luxuries and extras than one might have imagined.

Tip 4: define which costs are essential, and which are not

Identify every single expense of the couple and evaluate together if it is essential or not. Outgoing expenses such as rent, for example, will always be essential costs; other expenses, however, can be discussed together. Thus, you can plan your lifestyle to achieve a healthy balance between savings, investments, and daily expenses. And don't forget: Once you've categorized your expenses, they should stay in their own categories.

Tip 5: identify your long-term and short-term goals

Once you've established how much goes into your home, and how much you'll have to sacrifice for necessary expenses, you'll have a clearer idea of how much you can actually save. The next step is figuring out exactly what your long- and short-term goals are: You might want to buy a house, start saving for retirement, or plan a vacation. The important thing is that each goal is agreed together and planned in the budget.

Decide together a scale of priorities and how much money to allocate each month for each goal.

Tip 6: split the expenses

Each family member contributes differently to the needs of their family members. When one spouse earns more, however, in many cases a situation arises where the one who earns less feels in the position of contributing less to the growth of the family. Feelings of guilt or, worse, feeling this thing reproached end up inevitably compromising a marriage, speeding up its end more and more.

Depending on how you organize your finances as a couple, whether it's an account or joint bills, there are various ways to determine how each should contribute.

You can choose the simplest way and divide everything in half, perhaps based on the respective salary, or assign specific expenses to each one to divide the responsibilities for management and consumption. So, when allocating expenses, keep in mind who can contribute and how much, and set a figure that seems fair to both under the current circumstances. For couples with large income gaps, contributing 25% of each of their income towards expenses can create a more equitable financial climate.

Tip 7: invest your savings

Investing means making your savings pay off by choosing the most suitable instrument (government securities, bonds, shares, or customized investment plans). But investing also means thinking about retirement or insuring the family in time. In fact, once you have established your emergency account, your retirement account should be the first fund you entrust your savings to.

Tip 8: use the same approach when handling money

How a certain amount of money is handled can be a cause for discussion within a couple. Indeed, a certain aptitude for spending rather than saving can lead two spouses to conflict. Sporadic discussions can then become more and more frequent, especially when something is wrong or there is a specific need to meet.

Tip 9: monitor all purchases

Here's a common scenario: You're at the grocery store and your partner decides to buy some new jeans. You say no because you don't have cash available. The next day, he comes home with a brand-new pair of jeans that cost 100 euros.

To avoid this kind of situation, it's important to monitor all the couple's purchases. This means being aware of how much money you have in your account and making sure you don't spend more than you have available.

Tip 10: use technology to monitor your finances

Use online tools to track your spending and savings.

This isn't a new idea, but it's one we've seen time and time again: people who use technology in their financial lives are more likely to achieve their goals than those who don't. That's because technology gives us the ability to automate many tasks, such as saving for retirement or monitoring our spending habits (or even being warned when we're about to go over budget).

Week 3. How to improve intimacy as a couple

Intimacy is an essential part of the couple's harmony and planning. Satisfaction improves the relationship both with oneself and with the other by creating complicity with one's own corporeity.

It often happens that the couple goes through a moment of particular monotony, where everything flattens out. The motivations diminish. Desire seems to evaporate. It is, therefore, essential to introduce new emotions into familiar situations.

Therefore, it is not said that love is over, it could simply be the passing of the years that has caused boredom and habit to take over.

Stress, habit, tiredness, and boredom are all factors that negatively affect the couple's relationship. The negativity that often comes from the outside is vented at home where, over the months and years, it can turn into poison for the relationship. This strain can also seriously compromise the couple's sexual sphere, causing a decrease in desire on one or both sides. For this reason, some get caught up in doubt and suffering for fear that their partner no longer wants them, and this can further worsen the relationship, causing it to fall into a vicious circle.

In order to revive the relationship and rediscover the passion, it is necessary to understand if you are still attracted to your partner and, at the same time, try to pay more attention to details and experiment with new things.

Also, remember that communication is essential in these moments, but without letting go of recriminations.

Sexual desire does not derive from the act itself, but from a more general context that includes the partner's vision, his behavior, how valued and involved we feel, but also from every day and habitual aspects that tend to dampen creativity and seductive attitudes. For this reason, if in a general context, it is essential to work on communication, intimacy, and enhancement of the relationship and the partners involved, in the short term we can try to implement small tactics to awaken creativity and sensuality! Let's see some tips that can help rekindle the flame of passion in everyday life.

Tip 1: talk about the decline in desire

Communication is essential in the couple and talking about doubts and worries too, because it leads the other to realize what's going on. Perhaps by talking about it, you will discover that your partner feels the same thing, making you feel more accomplice and intimate.

So, take 30 minutes a day to talk: it's a classic exercise that is used a lot in couples therapy, easy and efficient. As we said before, as the couple becomes more mature, we tend to spend less time with our partner and above all to talk about what ails us.

The same goes for chats that are a healthy touch for the couple, especially for women who have a greater need to feel heard to reduce their stress.

Tip 2: take time just for you

Daily commitments, tiredness, and laziness tend to constantly invade the intimate and emotional sphere, so much so that it is often set aside in favor of something else. Instead, it is important to carve out a space for the couple, such as one evening a week dedicated to intimacy, sex, communication, or a dinner out, but which sees the couple at the center. Putting dates and times won't be very romantic, but it's the best way not to ignore taking care of something.

This part of the guide aims to provide indications to improve the intimacy and well-being of the couple. However, we must not forget that the couple is made up of two individuals with their individual needs and that it is also important to cultivate one's personal needs.

In the love relationship, when this reaches maturity, both the dimension of the individual and the dimension of the couple must be able to coexist.

In mature love the two polarities of "I" and "we" are not in a relationship of contradiction, competition or struggle, but enter into a harmonious relationship. When two people experience this type of love, there is a balance between "one" and "two", but it is not a static balance, but a dynamic balance in constant evolution.

There is a time to put yourself first and there is a time to put others first.

There are times when it's good to be alone and times when it's good to be together. There is the time to go and explore the world and there is the time to return home, as a couple.

Unfortunately, or fortunately, there are no fixed rules that allow you to always and, in every situation, identify whether to favor the individual dimension or the couple dimension. The balance between oneself and the couple is an art to be studied, practiced, and perfected throughout life.

Tip 3: change your approach

Obviously, after a long time, even sexuality can become less attractive if the same patterns are repeated over and over again. Try to get out of your rut and maybe try something new. This doesn't mean doing crazy things, but simply tackling things from another point of view or in another way.

Tip 4: communicate with your partner and talk about your fears and desires

Not talking about one's desires can only be detrimental to the couple and to the intimate sphere.

In addition to talking, it can be very useful to express what you want through body language and other elements or tricks. Music, games, clothing: everything can be useful for getting out of the routine and rediscovering something new. Between family, work and other commitments it is essential to carve out time for the couple, for example through a weekend alone at home or out of town. The important thing, after having spoken, is not to get caught up too much in rationality but rather to let go of one's desires, trying to communicate to the other what we like best. Not only the right place or clothing is enough, but it is necessary to try to find that lost understanding. For this, it is useful to go outside the box and surprise your partner.

The intimacy of a couple does not arise spontaneously, as one can often think, but it is a building, of constant research from a physical, psychological, and spiritual point of view. The intimacy of a couple is an art that comes from harmony and compatibility with each other. In this continuous and infinite research, it is essential to be able to communicate what one feels as one feels, to share joys and sorrows, and to live and plan a sentimentally, sexually, and spiritually true and profound present and future.

Tip 5: take care of your relationship by fighting boredom and monotony

Everyone knows that routine "kills relationships", but few know that "doing new things together" develops oxytocin, the substance that decreases stress and excites us when we are involved in new projects. Doing new things, even extremely small ones helps to solidify your bond.

Monotony can be unavoidable even for the most close-knit couples. It's also important to go back to taking care of yourself, not only to please your partner more but above all to feel good. Family life often tends to make us less attentive to our well-being and this situation also affects desire. Start playing sports, change your look, and give vent to your creativity through a new hobby. Getting out of the routine is useful not only for yourself but also for the couple. Start making new plans together again, like a long-desired trip or a dance class. Go back to dreaming together, not everything has already been done or said. Make it a habit to do something every month that interrupts the couple's routine. It can simply be a weekend away: two days in the mountains in winter in a remote cabin or two days in a farmhouse in spring.

If it is too expensive to travel outside the city, it might be enough to organize a dinner in your favorite restaurant. The goal is to carve out a "private" date just for the two of you.

Tip 6: make your partner feel special

We are human beings and as such we need to feel that we are important to the people who are important to us.

If we are convinced that our partner sees us, that he understands our feelings, our wants and needs, and that, consequently, he is willing to make sacrifices for our good, we feel "connected" and this translates into a sense of calmness and completeness. If, on the other hand, we feel that our partner is "disconnected", that he does not understand us and that he neglects us, the brain areas of emotions are activated intensely and send alarm signals.

Do something from time to time that communicates to your partner that is unique and special to you.

Each of us has his own way of feeling seen in his own uniqueness: there are those who need to hear words of love. There are those who need physical cuddles, kisses, and caresses. Who needs help with their difficulties. And who needs to receive gifts? And so on.

If you have no idea what makes your partner feel unique and loved, ask them, and use this information to create moments of togetherness and intimacy.

Tip 7: write a wish list

Sharing goals and projects unites us, and it is also an opportunity to dream together and make clear where we want to go together.

The Couple's Wish List also includes more modest wishes and projects or wishes that concern doing. Or, again, psychological desires: learning to respect and love each other even under stress, rediscovering the ability to have fun together, enjoy renewed emotional and physical intimacy.

It is important to talk about your desires with your partner, and decide together where you want to go together. And sanction the project of how you want the couple to be, reporting the common wishes in the Couple Wish List.

A tip: don't be too realistic, otherwise you'll limit the possibility of expressing your most hidden desires, of dreaming, of building castles in the air just like two children. Sometimes it is, in fact, nice to intentionally leave room for our childhood and dreamer side. And it's so much fun and intimate, doing it as a couple.

Finally, the Couple Wish List is not something that is done just once, rather it is a practice to be carried out periodically. It must therefore be an opportunity to take stock and identify what is important and where you want to go as a couple.

Tip 8: always celebrate your moments of connection

Sometimes the couple shares tears. In certain circumstances, moments with a great emotional charge are created in which one's fears, the most hidden difficulties, the darkest emotions, and the sense of guilt and shame that dwell in the depths of the psyche of all human beings are revealed to the other.

If in similar moments our partner welcomes us and loves us also for these aspects of our lives, those moments are indelibly stored in the psyche and, from that moment on, they will represent a treasure to be kept forever.

Those episodes of married life are remembered in dark circumstances and represent fundamental emotional resources, support, and consolation.

Such moments of the profound union must be celebrated, told to the partner, who may be unaware of their significance. Sharing these experiences with all the emotional components they convey creates and nurtures warmth and intimacy between partners.

Tip 9: increase physical contact

Holding hands more often, prolonging the kisses a little, getting closer when watching a movie on the sofa, or hugging each other for a while before sleeping. Don't let us forget each other's smell and touch. There is something strangely familiar about perfumes and it is often these that activate hormones. If we decide to share our life with another person, we make it as full and satisfying as possible.

Intimacy is a fundamental ingredient of married life and physical contact is its language. Without physical contact, the communication of love is so missing. There is a lack of gestures of affection, caresses, and sensations that cannot be discovered otherwise. Research has demonstrated the anti-stress, invigorating power of hugs and hand contact. Long walks hand in hand can help, as can hugging each other after a day's work.

Tip 10: try to see the positive sides of your partner every day

This ability goes against the trend of noticing what doesn't work in the partner and in the couple. Recognizing what you appreciate and love in each other, and using affirmations, appreciation, and love to convey that, paves the way for true intimacy.

We can start by asking ourselves how many times we tell our partner that we are happy that he/she is part of our life, or that "we like it". Then reflect on when was the last time, we expressed verbal appreciation for each other's actions. On the contrary, when was the last time we made a criticism? If the criticisms are more numerous than the appreciation, to improve the intimacy of the couple, it is necessary to learn to reverse the course.

Often couples, despite having years of an intimate relationship, show enormous difficulty in highlighting what qualities belong to their partner. They must think and rethink it before being able to list one or two qualities that, evidently, are made explicit without even too much conviction or by alluding to a defect connected to that same quality.

Week 4. How to handle the senseless fights of the couple

Sometimes couples experience problems that could be solved if both partners were able to change some of their personal ways of relating to each other. Moreover, often, almost without realizing it, the two partners slip into negative relationship models, or again fall into wrong personal habits, generating conflicts and discussions. Finally, to make the situation more complex is the stress to which we are subjected daily.

The "healthy" conflict, as we know, is a natural aspect; it helps to get to know each other and to develop intimacy, as it allows you to get to know yourself and your partner better, with their respective needs, stimuli, and motivations.

Love quarrels are a panacea for couple harmony. So, if we want to be happy, we just must fight. The important thing is that it is a peaceful conflict. Discussions are used to discuss and understand what needs to be done to improve the relationship, to continue building a satisfying and nourishing relationship without unpleasant backlash, where one of the partners seeks comfort elsewhere.

In a relationship it is important to have the courage to express your feelings to those you love, even if it is contrary to what the other feels. Swallowing, pretending that enduring for a long time without reacting will lead, sooner or later, to bursting, it will make even the most patient on the planet burn out.

But why do arguments arise in a couple's relationship? In addition to the differences between the two partners, arguments can arise due to problems external to the relationship. They can influence family problems, work-related problems, economic problems, or friendships that are not to the liking of one of the two partners. In addition, if we add cohabitation, it is logical that occasionally certain tensions are created which can give rise to quarrels.

Arguing every now and then is normal and necessary. It serves to clarify oneself, to find points of agreement and therefore to advance in the relationship. If you never argue, maybe one of you feels insecure and doesn't have the courage to express her opinion and this is not healthy at all. On the other hand, if the arguments are frequent and violent, then this is a pretty serious problem.

If we really want to know how to handle couple quarrels and use them to improve the relationship, we need to reach a point of agreement and reduce differences. Let's look at some strategies to achieve this.

Tip 1: start taking personal responsibility and apologizing if necessary.

The best thing to do to start smoothing out a couple of problems is to accept one's share of responsibility within the problem itself. Acknowledging your mistakes and taking responsibility, therefore, is the first critical step in resolving the conflict. One question you might ask yourself is, "What am I currently doing to make the situation worse, and what should I do to end the argument?" So instead of analyzing your partner's flaws, try to think about how your behavior contributes to perpetuating the problem. In some situations, in fact, we can decide to change the only thing that can be changed: ourselves.

In comparison, a person is not always right. If during the discussion one of the two realizes his error in assessment it is important to apologize. It doesn't mean being weaker, on the contrary, it will show the partner that it is important.

Tip 2: stop and start thinking about what you are doing or saying

Always give yourself time to stop and reflect on what you are saying. Stopping before giving your opinion can be very helpful when you feel too upset or are gripped by emotions such as anger or resentment. Know when to take a moment not to talk while allowing your partner to do the same. Let the other person take his time to think, when he comes back, most likely the tension level will not be so high.

During this pause, try not to focus on thoughts of indignation, victimization, or anger, rather, ask yourself: "What is the real problem for me? What do I want? How can I look at the problem from my partner's point of view? What would my partner like? What can I do to make the problem worse? What, however, is to solve it? How can I express myself more clearly?" In this way it is possible to try to get closer to your partner and speak with a different intention, with greater awareness and it will be easier, with an open mind and with awareness and willingness to try to understand each other.

Tip 3: don't blame each other

We are all capable of intentionally saying or doing unpleasant things to the people we love, particularly amid an argument and when feeling overwhelmed by negative emotions. In most cases, however, the reasons that trigger quarrels within a couple do not arise from negative intentions. Often, people are armed with good intentions but for this very reason, good intentions become the worst weapon to throw at your partner during an argument.

By starting to think this way, it will be easier to see your partner no longer as a "criminal" and to begin to think that whatever he said or did, the purpose of him had no negative intent. For example, suppose your spouse is doing his best to overcome a difficult situation and, due to fatigue, burns his dinner or ruins an object that you hold dear. Try to think that his intent was, despite his tiredness, to do something for you.

Tip 4: let go of the conflict even when you think the reason is on your side

The most frequent cause of quarrels is the belief that one is on the right side and that one's point of view is the correct one. You can feel frustrated if your partner disagrees with your opinion or if she has a different point of view. On the one hand, it is understandable that it is pleasant to be told you are right but, on the other hand, try to open your mind to begin to understand that, in a specular way, your partner also considers his personal point of view valid.

Try to give each other an open space for your partner's ideas, needs, and legitimate feelings. If you're not sure you understand what your partner is saying, ask him to explain himself better before making assumptions or jumping to the wrong conclusions.

Tip 5: learn to listen and avoid attacking

The most heated conflicts occur because one is often unable to listen to the other. Frequently, during a heated discussion, we are convinced that we are listening to the other, while, often, what happens is that we are "listening to ourselves", that is, we are thinking about what to say or how to counter the partner's arguments. The conflict will decrease in intensity if we, therefore, place ourselves in a condition of sincere listening to the other. Before expressing your opinion: - try to make a sort of summary of what the other has said - try to resist the urge to evaluate or analyze the "truth factor" in what your partner is saying. Emotions like pain, sadness, loneliness, and anger are neither right nor wrong. Just understanding them is an important first step in reducing tension.

When you find yourself raising an issue, try to do so by speaking clearly and directly about what your needs and perceptions are, instead of presenting the same thing, and attacking your partner (who can't help but hear the need to defend yourself).

Tip 6: leave the past behind

Leave the past in the past, otherwise, it invades the present and prevents the future. This is a fundamental aspect of a couple. The past is something that should be well placed in the memory box. Bringing it back to the surface is counterproductive and can only exacerbate the small misunderstandings or jealousies that may exist (don't forget that many come from previous ex experiences, often with children and someone to support). It's difficult because the past often resurfaces without us realizing it. The important thing is to block it immediately and not get carried away. Staying in the here and now is essential to give strength to the relationship and growth of both.

Tip 7: give appropriate time and space for the argument

Many quarrels occur under conditions where there is little time to discuss or there are other people present. This facilitates rash and impulsive expressions, or conversely escape and avoidance. An advantage of couple therapy is in fact that of allowing a well-defined space in which to face the conflict step by step, "vivisectioning" it, without the partners being able to avoid it by leaving or closing it with aggressive interventions, repeating the usual methods they adopt in daily life. Thus, even outside of therapy, it is necessary to establish a moment in which to discuss a problem; sometimes postponing the discussion to a later time can be the best choice if it is not a way to avoid the confrontation hoping that the matter will resolve itself spontaneously.

Tip 8: include the possibility of a time-out during your discussions

In quarrels, there is very often an escalation of tension up to a point of no return in which the interaction becomes destructive. In the couple, the same script is usually repeated, and it becomes quite easy for each of the partners to identify the stimulus that starts the escalation: it can be a certain phrase from the other or even just a particular look and gesture that " drives you crazy."

It then becomes useful to agree to establish a time-out moment as soon as one of the two realizes that the couple is implementing those dangerous stimulus-situations, to cool the climate. It may be a matter of physically moving away for a few minutes, moving to another room, or getting some fresh air in the garden, the important thing is that it is decided in a shared way and is, therefore, a constructive strategy to then discuss in a better way, and not an escape.

Tip 9: try to understand each other's feelings

Acknowledging them doesn't mean accepting or agreeing with them, but it does mean, "I understand you feel this way." It is a fundamental passage that is systematically disregarded, which -indeed- encounters strong resistance on the part of both, because each thinks that doing so would be tantamount to agreeing with the other, giving in, admitting they are wrong, justifying their own misconduct, to place oneself in a position of less power. Quite the opposite happens and recognizing each other's feelings allows two advantages. The first advantage is to lower the intensity of the conflict because when in a discussion we feel that the other, despite disagreeing with us, tries to put himself in our shoes and understand how we feel, our anger subsides. The second advantage is that it allows you to exhaust many discussions in which whoever expresses a problem is not looking for a solution or an answer but would just like to let off steam and be understood, as happens very often when a partner talks about a problem external to the couple and would just like to listen and understanding of one's state of mind, while the fact that the other proposes solutions to the problem triggers an argument with the accusation "Here, you don't understand me".

Tip 10: be careful how and when you express your opinions

Some modes of communication create irritation, and emotional activation interrupts listening by the other, fueling the quarrel. The most common mistakes are pointing out, recriminating, reproaching, the "I told you so" and "I'm only doing it for you". Try saying the same thing without resorting to these methods, you will be heard and understood better. Mutual listening is the basis of constructive dialogue, it is a prerequisite that allows us to arrive at a joint solution rather than a sterile confrontation. Try to analyze and carefully observe which communication mistakes you make most often and which communication mistakes often irritate your partner.

Also, remember that timing is everything. Paying attention to when to say something could help prevent a confrontation. Ask yourself when your partner is more sensitive to observations, when he is more tired or nervous, probably in these situations he is less available to listen.

Week 5. How to manage work and career

Work, as we know, is a bit of the black beast of couple relationships. First of all, because it is a source of stress and the latter, whether we like it or not, leads to quarrels, perhaps even over trifles. Furthermore, work is an obstacle to the full realization of the couple and of the relationship in another sense as well: being fulfilled at work sometimes leads to disagreements with the partner.

Professional achievement, therefore, has become one of those hot topics for the couple, as well as one of the root causes of divorce and quarrels. Like all problems, of course, this one is surmountable. Whether it's easy or not depends on the solidity of the couple. Surely, however, dialogue helps in any case: talk to your partner, expressing your doubts and perplexities regarding the career he is pursuing or aspires to have and point out to him the points that you believe could undermine your relationship.

Meeting your soul mate at work. Or decide to run a business together with your partner. Sharing career and private life requires great management skills, both practical and emotional. While on the one hand making the line between intimacy and professionalism disappear can have harmful effects, on the other it is also true that sharing professional dynamics can promote understanding. Sharing your private life and professional career with your partner seems impossible, but you just need to follow a few small rules so as not to ruin the understanding.

Tip 1: avoid having lunch together

It's important to carve out spaces to cultivate your individuality. If you live in symbiosis with your partner, the topics of conversation may fail. Going to lunch in different places or with other colleagues can certainly be a great way to preserve one's professional sphere... and to know what to talk about in the evening at dinner. An alternative solution may be to go to work from time to time by different means, perhaps taking advantage of some errands that force you to make a detour on the way home to the office.

Tip 2: treat yourself to a day of relaxation without talking about work

Defining a time of day when you can talk about everything, except work, can be an opportunity to take a break from professional life and focus on the couple. Setting rules is important, but sometimes it can be crucial.

Tip 3: maintain decorum and professionalism

Don't let a romantic relationship affect the quality and efficiency of your work. You don't have to keep your relationship a secret, but you also don't have to show it off in a way that makes coworkers feel uncomfortable.

Consider the fact that colleagues may be looking for your mistakes. You would never want a co-worker to think, "Joan is only okay with Claudio's plan because they're dating." Avoid sitting next to each other in meetings, having lunch together every day, or generally acting as a couple. Also, do not send personal messages using work email or company chats.

Keep your roles distinct and never act as a partner to other employees: this attitude will negatively affect your authority and, even worse, your professionalism.

Tip 4: Never mix private life and career together

Quarrels, jealousy, and spite are not allowed in front of employees or even worse, customers. If you have spent the night yelling and throwing dishes at each other, this must absolutely not leak at work, rather reserve the second round for the following evening.

Tip 5: try not to compete

Sharing a profession is only possible if there are no competitive dynamics between the two spouses: wanting to excel at all costs, enhancing one's own qualities by belittling (even unintentionally) those of the partner, these attitudes not only risk creating disagreements within the company, but they profoundly lower the partner's self-esteem, inevitably leading to a break in the couple

Tip 6: learn to manage stress levels due to your work situation

In the short term, a situation of this type with high work stress affects the relationship with forgotten or canceled appointments, quarrels, and lack of communication with the partner. If your relationship is healthy and strong, your partner will be understanding and try to get you to open up about what's going on. For your part, you must try to be aware of the phase you are going through and identify the source of the stress. You'll need to be able to confide in your partner about what you're going through at work and why you're often nervous or angry. It's important that you build this trusting relationship with the person you share your life with. To get your partner to support you, you need to be willing to come up with a strategy to improve the situation and communicate it to the other so that they calm down.

Tip 7: learn to balance work and private life

In many cases, stress is part of the job, you can't get rid of it. For this reason, you and your partner must learn to manage its effects within the relationship. It's important that you learn to compartmentalize so that you know how to confine work-related stress and worries to just the workplace. I know these are always said but it is essential to take care of yourself to decompress in daily life. So, start right from the basics: move a little every day, don't sacrifice hours of sleep, and take time to do something that nourishes you and makes you feel good.

Tip 8: don't hide your worries and work problems

Hiding from your life partner that you are having problems at work or having a hard time is not good for your relationship. You miss out on creating a moment of emotional connection with him. On the other hand, even complaining and venting to your partner by monopolizing the conversation and using him as an outlet valve will in the long run lead your partner to move away, also because he will feel unable to help you.

Let him know what you need. "I would like some advice" or "I have to get rid of this weight" are effective ways in which you can communicate your needs to others and make sure that they are met. Try not to be the center of attention all the time with your problems at work and the desire to let off steam. Don't forget to take a genuine interest in the person you love and ask him how his day was. It seems obvious, but when you're in a hyper-stress phase, you forget about it, because there's only you with your problems. And your partner feels it. Let him know that, despite everything, you are there for him, just as he is ready to support you. This will strengthen your bond even more.

Tip 9: trust each other

Mutual trust also comes into play between engaged couples, husbands and wives, and partners who work together. If we trust the other, in fact, on the one hand, we can leave room for his decisions and his point of view with respect to the project or commercial activity that we manage together.

On the other hand, we can prepare ourselves to accept the partner's possible disagreement and his assessments of his own work with more serenity.

Tip 10: don't change your plans

Love should never interfere with our work plans, not even love born at work. If the relationship were to start it would be very important to distinguish the plans, your behavior in the office cannot be distorted, intimacy must be left outside the company door. This avoids contaminating the surrounding environment, but above all, it won't make you lose sight of your career goals.

Week 6. How to manage social relationships

One of the secrets to creating a successful couple relationship is keeping sociability alive.

When love arrives, many are inclined not to share their free time with friends, frequently falling back into social isolation.

Love, especially in the first phase, confuses us and makes us think that the only way to be happy and complete is to share our every breath with our loved ones. In these phases, we only think that, by spending every moment of our life with our loved one, we can be truly happy.

In reality, we must be careful, because we must not run the risk of attributing a saving power to our partner as little by little, we can start by losing our self-esteem, our essence, and personal wealth.

The secret is to understand, from the first moment, that in relationships it is necessary to maintain three interconnected poles: the couple and the individuality. By taking care of these three elements at the same time, we will have the certainty that we are laying the foundations so that our relationship can maintain energy and happiness intact over time, and therefore, preventing some problems in the couple's relationship, and at the same time avoiding throwing into the couple our frustrations by continuing the process of individual growth.

When someone enters our lives everything changes, the social and individual balances built and conquered over the years change. For many, this change is experienced as a renunciation, especially by those who have not been in a stable relationship for several years.

It is not a question of giving up our previous life or our old friends, but of working so that our old world not only welcomes the new person who is at our side positively but that harmony is created between them.

Obviously, all this in words seems very simple, but we must not let ourselves be discouraged and be aware that these are not immediate and sudden processes. Most of the time small steps and constant work are required.

Here are some tips on how to better manage social relationships.

Tip 1: take care of your individuality

We often forget that love is born at the moment in which we are single individuals and that it was precisely that personality that gave birth to the spark; therefore, we must always preserve and not give up those elements that make us unique.

To be healthy, love must be seen as enrichment, empowerment, and completion, the other completes us, and does not overwhelm, or cancel us, rather it highlights and amplifies our peculiarities.

We must therefore resist the temptation to adapt our personality to how he/she wants us to be because in this way it is inevitable that a time bomb will be triggered which over time is destined to explode.

From this point of view, especially when you realize that this time "is the right one", you need to keep individual interests alive and be able to carve out moments in which you take care of yourself. In this way, we will avoid incumbent in the problem of channeling all our happiness exclusively into the life of a couple and of creating mechanisms of frustration.

For this, don't be afraid to see your friends and family even alone, to continue to cultivate your hobbies and practice your favorite sport. In the medium to long term, this suffering that is created by the separation from one's partner for a few hours will be the way to prevent more or less serious problems in the couple. Thus, at the same time, you will always ensure a shoulder to cry on or confide secrets that only a friend or family member can keep.

Tip 2: go gradually

Of course, introducing your partner to all your friends, in a single meeting, can be comfortable, but potentially disastrous: maybe he could feel too much at the center of attention, or overwhelmed by too many new acquaintances, without having the opportunity to establish a real connection with anyone. Start by introducing your partner to your best friend or best friend, or at least the most outgoing and trusting one, who will then help you gradually introduce them to the rest of the group. Or start organizing an aperitif or dinner with a handful of closest friends: once the ice is broken, it will be easier to stay in company.

Tip 3: Make your friends accept your partner

There would be no need to have our partner accept our friends, but it is not always easy to manage all the various emotions and the various types of love and affection. Our friends were there before him, they were with us at various points in our lives and helped us through difficult times. Therefore, when a stranger arrives and demands to join our group, he should do so calmly trying to be accepted. There is the one who tries to please, the one who is too shy and stays in the rear, but the need to be accepted remains. For our part, however, it is important to find the right compromise between our life before and our new relationship.

Tip 4: avoid your relationship from becoming all-encompassing

The idea of all-encompassing love, a person who becomes "your everything", is very poetic, but let's face it: it's not very healthy.

It's not good for us to live the relationship like a cage, actually, it should make us feel freer than ever. It's good for everyone to disconnect a little and it shouldn't be seen as something negative, or as an escape from the relationship, it's normal freedom that makes us feel good and allows us to breathe deeply. It is this space that everyone dedicates to themselves that allows them to live well within the relationship without being crushed by it.

Do you feel like your partner wants to hang out with his friends too often? Or do you feel guilty because sometimes you find yourself having to "abandon" your better half? Always remember that friends are part of your life, but also his.

Is this little remainder not enough for you? Here are 2 useful tips: introduce him/her to your friends, by doing so you will be able to maintain your group of friends and have an extra point of sharing, furthermore your partner will be more willing, having established a relationship with them, when you tell him that you are going out in company; create new friendships together, a new group of friends can push you to new experiences and strengthen the bond between you. This way you will manage not to lose friends for love, let alone the love for friends!

Tip 5: try to find the right balance

The key is to strike a healthy balance between the two parties, and that might be easier said than done. When trying to scale some relationships, you need to consider your work schedule, your family needs, and all your other day-to-day commitments, and you need to be careful not to overlook anything but the minor. For example, if as a single person, you go out with friends three to five nights a week, and then suddenly stop altogether, someone is bound to get hurt.

In these cases, if you want to spend the evenings with your partner because he works during the day, try to carve out time for a coffee, lunch, or weekend brunch with friends. There is a way to manage and keep your friends in your life so that no one feels left out because of their partner.

Friendships are often taken for granted, and we think our friends can understand why we choose them. As if everyone were in our heads, as if they all thought like us as if we don't suffer when the same happens to us. When we have a new partner, one might think that we have everything we need, but the reality is that "lifelong companions" can offer us even more.

Tip 6: try to make friends and social relationships a priority as such in your relationship as a couple.

Try to plan days or times within the week to be devoted exclusively to social relationships. Try to keep these scheduled appointments without ever canceling because something to do with your partner crops up at the last minute. Prioritizing social relationships is a good way to keep both your relationship and your relationship with others stable. Isolating yourself completely to be alone with your partner will soon bring boredom and monotony into your life and forever wear out your relationship.

Tip 7: give your attention to the needs of others

When you spend time with your friends or family outside of your relationship, try to give them your full attention.

When you are out with other people, try to put your relationship aside for a moment, avoid continuous calls or texts, and devote your attention to the people who are there with you. Also, look for topics of conversation that affect everyone, and stop talking all the time and incessantly only about your partner. So, make sure you have adequate conversation time that concerns you and then dedicate the same time to your friends. Everyone must feel listened to and not monopolized.

Tip 8: try to make your partner understand the benefits of social relationships

Talk to your partner about the benefits of maintaining social relationships and the need to connect with other people outside of your relationship.

Even if your relationship is very stable and you are very happy to always be together, if you feel the need to have relationships outside, with your family or friends it is right that you talk about it with your partner and try to find a compromise. For example, you can tell your partner that you really enjoy spending all that time together but that it could be beneficial for both of you to also spend some time apart to do essential things, such as shopping or going out for an evening with your friends.

Tip 9: involve your partner in hanging out with groups of other friends more often.

The dynamics of large groups of friends can be complicated to manage, but if you create a good friendship then going out together often and organizing trips and evenings out can be as fun and fulfilling as being together alone with your partner.

Planning group activities, therefore, involves going out together with your friends and your partner at the same time. An important tip to keep social relationships alive in these cases is to not only pay attention to your partner but also to socialize with group members.

Tip 10: try to be available and always respond to messages, calls or emails from your relatives and friends.

Being in a love relationship does not give you the authorization to shut off any kind of communication with the outside world. The excuse that you were too busy to answer not only doesn't hold up, but it is very offensive towards those who, for all the time you needed, have always been available to you. So, try to reply regularly to your friends or relatives when they contact you, especially if they need advice or help. Thanks to the digitization and development of social media, it will not be difficult for you to devote time to social relationships without necessarily having to neglect your partner.

Week 7. How to manage extra-work activities as a couple

Generally, the initial phase of a couple's relationship is characterized by a great euphoria, linked to the fact that everything that happens is new. The first walk together, the first kiss or the first ice cream, the surprises, and attentions of the partner.

It's very common that, over time, love relationships fall back into routine: get up, take the dog out, go to work, and come back in the evening. Having done all this, how much time do you have left for fun, and what happened to the spontaneity you had at the beginning of your relationship as a couple?

Sure, if you've been a couple for a while now, it's been a while since you've shared time together, just the two of you, hand in hand, heart to heart. Children, home, and work have taken up so much time and now you just need to carve out a corner just for you.

Certainly, there is no doubt that you love to death, but everyday life completely fills your heart and head, to the point of never being able to find the time to organize a moment of special sharing with your partner. Drop everything and take some quality time, all you need is to organize a special evening to spend time with your partner.

We know that intimacy with your partner is cultivated through self-disclosures, interactions, conversations, and, of course, shared experiences.

Trying to dedicate more time to you as a couple, trying new experiences and unforgettable moments, can only lead to a positive improvement in your relationship. To do all this you don't need a lot of free time or spending absurd amounts of money. Simple activities carried out together or small romantic gestures are equally useful for improving your bond as a couple.

Tip 1: try something new

After a stressful day at work, both at home and outside, a good way to strengthen your relationship and get out of the usual routine could be the "anything can happen Thursday". The basic idea is taken from the well-known TV show Big Bang Theory, but instead of doing something new only on the third Thursday of the month, you can try your hand at experimenting with something new, such as going to the cinema, taking a course together, every Thursday evening after having done all your chores.

Tip 2: Plan a relaxed day after work for just the two of you.

The ideal would be to organize a whole day in a spa and completely relax for a weekend after spending a whole week between work, children, and various commitments.

However, if time is not enough for you, you can organize an evening, or an entire spa day, even at your home.

To have an atmosphere that is as close as possible to that of a spa, first of all, you have to imagine that you are right there: in a spa, there are no telephones ringing, or disturbing noises; therefore, it is necessary to isolate oneself a little from the world to avoid distractions or sources of stress.

Obviously, absolute silence is not contemplated, so you can choose background music that is as appreciated as possible, but that is rigorously calm.

The candles create a very relaxing and romantic soft light. They can be placed in the bathroom away from towels or electrical sockets, placed near the bathtub, for example. Scented candles will help to release an intoxicating smell: however, it is better to choose similar aromas to create a pleasant olfactory experience.

You can then take a relaxing bath together with perfumed oils and aromas that invite you to relax and release the tensions accumulated after an incessant and stressful working day.

Tip 3: an infallible classic, a romantic dinner at home

To organize a romantic dinner at home, you don't need to be a star chef; there are so many recipes that can be found online with which you can experiment with your culinary skills. But if the stove scares you or you're too tired to cook, even a takeaway dinner enjoyed by candlelight and accompanied by a good wine in the privacy of your home will be a pleasant and romantic surprise that will warm your partner's heart. Wear elegant clothes, light up the spaces with scented candles, choose the right music, and don't forget to do things with a little style: after all, very little is needed.

Tip 4: host a game night

Whether they are board games, cards, or video games, treat yourself to an evening of challenges and fun. Do you want to make this playful evening even more exclusive and personalized? Then you create the activity, perhaps creating a quiz with a series of questions related to your love story, with special prizes up for grabs, spicy or romantic, the choice is yours.

Tip 5: organize an evening dedicated only to you and to music

From karaoke in your car to concerts of your favorite band, there are so many moments you've shared to the rhythm of music, and if it seems like forever since you've attended a concert, well it's time to fix. Take a look at the music programs in your city or in the places where you are planning a weekend away, and buy two tickets for a live performance, a DJ set or a concert that you are happy to see for the first time, or review for the umpteenth time.

Tip 6: do not plan anything but leave everything to improvisation

Partners in life but also partners in crime: you are a couple who never back down from adventures and improvisation is your specialty, in your case don't organize an evening but let it create itself. Leave the monotony of the daily routine at home and start your evening simply by taking a car and driving without a specific destination, or by walking down the street being inspired by what is happening around you. Who knows what adventures fate has in store for you?

Tip 7: organize an evening dedicated to your passions

If you know your love well then you will also know what his great passions are. To organize a special evening, you can start with the things he loves the most. Sports enthusiasts, for example, will be happy to watch an important match whether it's football, tennis or basketball, or movie lovers will feel in heaven in front of a giant screen and a family-sized pack of popcorn. In short, whatever his great passion is, with an evening dedicated to the latter you will certainly impress.

Tip 8: dedicate a romantic evening to dinner in a starred restaurant.

Look for a nice and refined restaurant for your special evening, which maintains an intimate and secluded atmosphere, and which boasts a dessert menu that can send your taste buds into ecstasy. The evening doesn't necessarily have to end there, choose where to make love, if it's been a while since you last did it in the car why not take advantage of this place after many years, you will feel as if you were catapulted into that period where it was the only place to be alone.

Tip 9: throw a party to celebrate everything you've been through together

Just as you can recall your childhood or your life "before", you can bring out photos from the beginning of your relationship.

This way, you can retrace your journey together and mark the important moments. Also, you can create your own version of the "Two Truths, One Lie" game.

Tip 10: Choose a new interest to do together

While it's important for a couple to have their own personal space, it's also essential that they have something in common.

So, if you want to have a nice romantic evening, try to find an interest that you both like and start this activity right away.

Not only will you spend quality time together, but you can also learn together.

Week 8. How to manage free time as a couple

At some point, even the most active and close-knit couple can feel a bit bored or used to it.

Even if you've been a couple for a long time, that doesn't mean you have to spend your evenings and weekends at home in front of the TV.

We often don't devote as much time to our partner as we would like. It is as if work sucked all our energies; therefore, once we get home, going out again is the last thing we want to do. However, without either of them realizing it, this situation causes a sort of detachment in the couple. If not noticed in time, it can become the start of a long series of problems. Choosing an activity to do as a couple could be an excellent solution to solve the problem.

Unfortunately, or fortunately, not everyone happens to have the same tastes as their partner. Sometimes having nothing in common can even be uplifting, but sometimes it ends up being a real nuisance.

Of course, every relationship has its ups and downs, but pursuing a hobby together can be a good strategy to help the former outweigh the latter. Surely, among the wide choice of activities that can be carried out, there will be one or more than one that can be liked and can be carried out by both. The important thing is not to have prejudices about what to do or not, also because trying new things will give you the opportunity to learn something you haven't taken into consideration yet.

The advantages of doing an activity as a couple are immense. Doing something together in your free time will help you feel more united, it will help you get to know each other better, making your bond stronger. Involving one of the two partners outside of everyday life can actually be the solution to your problems. Sharing a hobby or activity outside of work and outside of marriage with your partner will help you spend more time together. Practicing a hobby together favors the maintenance of a certain complicity which is often lost due to routine.

A hobby shared by both of you will increase your complicity and help you connect. These are two essential elements for building a healthy couple relationship that must never be underestimated. Furthermore, this new understanding can also help you strengthen intimate relationships with your partner.

Furthermore, practicing an activity together is a good way to unleash your creativity and defeat the boredom that often leads to the definitive breaking of a bond.

Practicing a hobby in the company is always more fun than doing it alone. In fact, it has been scientifically proven that practicing activities together with your partner makes us much happier than doing the same activity alone. Obviously, this is not an invitation to practice sports or leisure activities exclusively with your partner. We all need some moments of solitude, it is undeniable. But it is equally undeniable that doing things together allows us to see what we are doing from another point of view, making us discover aspects of what we are doing that we had never noticed before.

Tip 1: take courses in creative writing

Creativity is important in relationships. Then, go to a writing class and exchange ideas with each other.

You will end up having a lot of fun and you will probably learn something new about your partner.

Writing isn't something that many people tend to do, making it a fun and interesting thing to try as a couple.

Tip 2: go dancing together

Regional dances, tango, salsa, and bachata, all styles are valid if they help you connect with your partner. Through dance, you can establish a strong emotional connection with your partner, something you can achieve by taking lessons or simply letting the rhythm wash over you.

Tip 3: go camping

Camping gives both of us a chance to get off the grid and spend some time away from the real world.

Make it a regular occurrence and set some rules e.g., no phones before bedtime so you can enjoy the stargazing.

Tip 4: take cooking lessons

Cooking classes are an adorable way to make something otherwise mundane really fun.

You will prepare many new dishes - there are special menus that you can choose if you want to learn the art of sushi, for example.

This is a perfect hobby for couples as you will be able to eat your meals throughout the day and bring home some new ideas for dinner time.

Cooking a meal together can be a lot of fun for couples. There's no doubt that every chef needs an assistant, and your partner can provide the help you need. When you cook, you both can learn by teaching each other new tricks.

Tip 5: dedicate yourself to hiking

There's nothing like getting outside and enjoying the fresh air.

The hiking is physical enough that you both feel like you've accomplished something by the time you reach the top of the mountain or the end of the trail. It will also give you a chance to help each other out which is a healthy way to strengthen your relationship.

Tip 6: take holidays and trips as a couple

Discovering new places and relaxing together will allow you to get out of the daily routine, help rekindle the romance and give you a chance to find each other again, especially if things weren't working so well lately.

There is no need to go very far or organize a super trip to enjoy this experience to the fullest; consider going to the countryside or to a nearby village where you can get away from the city air for a while.

If you are an adventurous person, a weekend in nature to discover hidden places could be the right choice for you.

If, on the other hand, you prefer something more peaceful, making a list of places and cities you would like to visit and slowly completing it could be the right compromise. Not only will it allow you to visit places you've always wanted to see, but you could do it in the company of your favorite person.

Tip 7: do a DIY

Crafting can be a great activity to do as a couple. Whether it's for small jobs around the house, or to unleash your creativity, it doesn't matter. Choosing materials and tools as a couple, leafing through catalogs, and collaborating in the creation of a small project can only revive the couple and make you spend fun moments together.

Tip 8: read together

Starting a book together with your partner will certainly be fun. If you both love reading, it will be a good way to spend time together, especially in winter when you spend more time indoors. You could perhaps recite the dialogues of the text or take turns reading so as not to get bored and make everything more pleasant.

Tip 9: decorate a room together

Many couples live together, but their home is not a reflection of their union, but rather of their coexistence. The best way to change this is to turn a room into a place that represents your love.

Furnishing a room together, choosing the furniture, the color of the walls, the floor, the paintings... is the best way to represent the personality of your bond, which is more than the sum of two people, it is a sign of identity.

Tip 10: Exercise together

Exercising together will motivate you to be more disciplined and enable you to adopt a healthier lifestyle.

Both of you can make the decision to follow a healthy eating plan and exercise routine at the gym or at home. In fact, this habit will serve to reinforce everything that has to do with moments of intimacy.

Several studies have shown that couples who exercise together are more satisfied with their relationship than those who do not.

Going for a run, going for a walk, going to the gym, or finding a partner sport are some of the options that could benefit your relationship. Training together will contribute to your understanding and will also increase the passion under the covers, putting a little spice in your intimate sphere.

Playing sports with your partner will not only improve your relationship but will also increase your personal motivation, allowing you to reach the desired goal more likely.

Week 9. How to improve romance as a couple

In a long-standing couple, it is sometimes necessary to reawaken lost romance; it's not about having to make big gestures but transforming some simple actions into routine habits.

Sometimes we forget how important it can be to make our partner feel appreciated.

For this, it is necessary to translate what we feel into actions, without spending a fortune or indulging in blatant demonstrations of affection.

Surely passion and desire are important feelings within a relationship, but studies show that lately, couples prefer to indulge in the most romantic pleasure, namely that of simply being together. Which in our times seems almost a utopia. Unfortunately, in fact, the frenetic pace of our society has a negative impact on the time you can spend with your partner. Everyday problems tend to make the couple's relationship more tense and full of misunderstandings. But don't be discouraged: it's the quality time you spend together that matters.

Romanticism is made up of details, it is the details that are then attributed to other connotations. But then why is it so difficult to be romantic? It seems that at a certain point, the fear of romanticism began and that is the fear of falling into the banal, but romantic does not necessarily mean banal or vice versa, like all things it just needs balance. The difference between trivial and romantic is fiction, a gesture that is made to garner admiration rather than making the loved one feel special is trivial. Or many fantastic and refined words to impress when what matters is simply expressing what you feel with sincerity. These details make any moment truly unique; they are important moments that remain etched in a person's memory forever. So much so that it can flourish again at any time, even after many years.

Tip 1: awaken romance by starting the day with a romantic gesture

Every morning you should start the day with a smile: and what better way than with an affectionate and romantic gesture?

Whether you live together or are still just engaged, there is always a way to let each other know how much we love them.

A couple living together can start the day with a cuddle in bed. Dedicate a few minutes to kisses and hugs before getting up, and if you have extra time, dedicate it to some more intense cuddles. Turning this pleasant ritual into a routine will help you start the day in the best way, focusing all the attention on your partner during the day.

If, on the other hand, you sleep in two separate houses, you can send a good morning message as soon as you wake up, or - even better - by calling your partner as soon as possible. Talking together is a great way to start the day right, making it clear to our partner that you are always a priority compared to the other commitments of the day.

Tip 2: awaken romance with unexpected gifts

The gift is very often a routine task, limited exclusively to Christmas and special occasions. Instead, try to surprise your partner with an unexpected gift, any day of the year.

A small thought, like a flower or breakfast in bed, is enough to pleasantly surprise the person you love. In this way, the gift will have greater value because you did it without any "compulsion" and without any double purpose. This little trick serves not only to awaken romance but to keep it always alive and lively. Again, no blatant or expensive gestures are needed: bringing breakfast to bed is a sweet (and free) way of dedicating extra attention to the person you love.

Tip 3: keep sexuality alive

The fourth and final piece of advice not to be forgotten is to always keep sexuality alive by also consolidating your physical relationship. Tease your partner with compliments or provocative jokes and indulge in small transgressions.

The physical aspect of a relationship is extremely important and should not be forgotten.

Especially in long-standing couples, this aspect tends to fade over time, leaving the initial attraction to a period of flat stability.

Sometimes (unfortunately) the couple forgets to find the time to keep sexuality alive. Work, family, children, and housework transform sex into just another physical task to be completed in the shortest possible time. Rediscover romance by carving out precious time. No matter how tired you are, never forget to value the sexual aspect.

Make your partner feel desirable and always loved, taking care of them physically and psychologically. Rediscovering sexual understanding will give new life and new energy to the relationship, making your relationship even healthier and more dynamic.

Tip 4: make a fixed appointment

Stopping courting is a serious mistake but routine sometimes takes over without you realizing it. So how to keep love alive? You can make yourself a promise: allow yourself a fixed appointment, every month, every three months, or whenever you want if you establish it at the beginning of your life as a couple. Choose a day when, regardless of everything and everyone, you will wear the best elegant wedding dress to dedicate yourself exclusively to each other.

Tip 5: only fall asleep after a goodnight kiss

It may be obvious, but it is not at all. In reality, this advice is linked to another: never go to bed without making peace. Always reconcile even if it takes a whole night. Impose it as an indispensable point for your life as a couple.

Tip 6: Visit the place where you first met.

Romantic gestures like this are a beautiful way to remember the precious moments you have shared with your partner. You could go to the place where you first met or the place where you first kissed, or where she said "I love you" for the first time.

Tip 6: visit the place where you first met

Romantic gestures like this are a beautiful way to remember the precious moments you have shared with your partner. You could go to the place where you first met or the place where you first kissed, or where she said "I love you" for the first time.

Tip 7: write a letter

Yes, and by this we don't mean a message through social networks, WhatsApp, or email. We are referring precisely to a letter written in your hand, it doesn't matter how the important thing is that it is something written by you. You will be able to take the opportunity to put into words the happiness you feel and how lucky you feel to have the other person in your life; you will be able to retrace the happy moments spent together or more simply, describe how important it is to you, giving words that spring directly from your heart.

The important thing is the return to this millenary habit when couples who lived a long-distance love affair had no choice but to live an epistolary relationship and, despite having to wait months for an answer, this was awaited with enthusiasm and happiness.

Tip 8: plan a romantic date

There are thousands of options, try to get away from traditionalism and daily routine. In fact, it can happen that when you have been together for a long time, you forget the importance of sharing romantic and unforgettable moments. So, organize an evening as you did in the early days of the relationship, think of a romantic place, invite her to dinner, take a walk hand in hand under the moonlight, perhaps remembering your most romantic moments.

An unexpected romantic evening will take you out of your routine and strengthen your relationship thanks to the quality time you will spend together.

Tip 9: give your partner something made by you

We often focus on expensive gifts: the designer watch she wanted, the latest smartphone, or the perfume she's always wanted. However, for an unexpected date or any day, you could surprise your partner by giving them something made by you. A ticket, coupons for kisses or hugs, an invitation to the cinema or a bike ride, a photo album that contains your most important moments.

Tip 10: remind yourself every day why your partner is the love of your life

It's never too much. Whether it's with a note or face to face, when you wake up next to them or before sleep, remind your partner how much they mean to you, how much you love them, how important they are in your life, and how happy you are to be able to be with them every day. Sometimes we forget how important and essential these details are for the success of the relationship.

They say that words are carried away by the wind, nevertheless, they must be said, we must express what we have inside, and take advantage of every moment we have next to the person we love. For this, go back to those moments when paying a compliment to your partner was something usual, this will always keep the flame of love burning.

Week 10. How to best manage cohabitation

During a relationship, there comes that moment when you start thinking about living together. There are those who fear it, those who await it with joy and those who see it as a prerogative for marriage. In any case, sharing the same house is a very important step in the life of any couple. However, one naturally wonders when the time has come to be able to do it in serenity, without risking the relationship getting worse, and how it is possible to be able to live together well, avoiding unnecessary tension or quarrels.

There is no single sign that warns us that the time has come to move in with your partner. There are several, which may vary from case to case. There are couples who feel ready to live together after a few months of a relationship, while others take several years. However, it is not the time behind a love story that is the only important factor. In fact, before going to live together, you need to know if that's exactly what you want and if you feel ready to make this change within the relationship.

Moving in together means planning the future together. We must be very honest on this point because it is essential to understand whether coexistence is desired by both parties. If you and your partner are always making long-term plans that involve both of you and you always see each other over the years, then moving in together won't be as scary as many think.

Remember, however, that moving in together must be a desire for both and not a force: thinking of sharing the same house just to please the other is not only wrong but proves to be counterproductive within a few days of your living together.

If living together must be a shared decision, in the same way, external pressures on your couple must not take over: seeing only the economic advantage of dividing expenses or the mere desire to leave the family of origin are not enough reasons to embark on this path.

Once you have established that the time has come to move in together, it is good that you keep in mind some advice for peaceful coexistence.

Tip 1: carefully choose the house where you are going to live together

One of the first rules for peaceful coexistence must be applied even before coexistence begins: we are talking about choosing a home.

Usually, this is quite automatic if one of the two owns a house while the other is renting. The solution is quite immediate, also because it is the most practical and the most cost-effective. The only contraindication: establish well at the beginning how to manage expenses, especially if the homeowner is bearing the costs of the mortgage.

Similar speech if both live in rent, but one of the two houses is suitable for life as a couple: in this case, the contingencies have been chosen for you.

But what if you both have your own home? The answer is unpopular: choose a third home, perhaps rented, which meets the needs of both, and which represents a neutral territory.

Another important issue is space: living together in confined spaces can become problematic, especially in the event of quarrels, but not only. Consider spending a little more obviously if possible and look for a home that allows everyone to have the space of hers.

Tip 2: establish early on how to manage expenses

We know that in the throes of joy and euphoria that one feels before moving in together, little thought is given to the economic factor. However, in everyday life, it presents itself constantly and cannot be overlooked. Even before arriving in the new house, decide how to divide the expenses. Our advice is to try to divide them in half, obviously without exaggerating with precision and counting the single cent.

Dividing expenses equally gives you a way not to depend too much on your partner and to feel both responsible for yourself and for your life as a couple. Start dividing up the various bills, while for smaller expenses, use the classic "list" where everyone writes something down or the innovative apps that are perfect for keeping accounts in the family.

Remember that, in any family partnership, your attitudes towards money will have a strong impact on the future of both of you. That's why conversations about money and spending are essential if you're planning to live together.

Tip 3: establish early on how to handle cleaning and household chores

Cohabitation between two people is a sort of partnership, and for this reason, one must be willing to share responsibilities as well. Sharing responsibilities like chores around the house, and planning ahead about how to handle them, will help prevent resentments related to feeling exploited by either partner.

It is the same problem as the economic aspect: before starting to live together you don't think about it, but sharing the same roof also means sharing the various tasks of managing the house. The best way is to decide equally which household chores you do and which you will do. Obviously, preferences can be expressed that could be to the advantage of both. Maybe you just can't stand ironing, but he doesn't mind it so much. Conversely, your partner's weak point is cleaning the kitchen when it's a normal household routine for you. As always, the keyword compromise and a little willingness to collaborate are useful.

Good compromises can be not focusing too much on how the other does the cleaning, dividing the tasks based on the ones we like best to complete, but also deciding to hire a domestic collaborator.

Tip 4: face the difficulties of living together by communicating

Living together also means growing up. Who has never had an argument with their partner that was followed by several days of silent treatment towards each other? It happens often, but it can only occur when the couple does not live together and can take their space within their respective homes before clarifying with the partner.

If you have chosen to move in together, you must know that this will no longer be possible. Not talking to your partner for hours if not days following a fight will only create a really unpleasant atmosphere and obvious tension in the home. When there is a difficulty, one must open up to confrontation and dialogue. If there's something bothering you about your partner, don't withdraw into yourself but tell him about it: this is the only way to prevent an even more difficult quarrel and restore serenity to your home.

By getting to know each other, a large part of the job will be to prevent fights. But this does not mean avoiding conflict at all costs: the confrontation must be frank and must not overflow. If something bothers you, always say it and discuss it: it's a great way to defuse a possible much more serious rift.

Tip 5: Create a couple of space

To be able to live together, we must accept a certain invasion of our intimacy, of our space; you must learn to create a new space, as a couple. Share wishes and plans for the future. Love is truly capable of anything; it can be considered the universal glue because it unites what breaks. However, one must be aware that breaks, however small, leave traces; it is, therefore, necessary to avoid hurting each other, especially when the reason that triggered the disagreement is small for both.

Tip 6: respect each other's habits

Sharing the same house makes you discover things about each other that you would never have imagined. He eats too late compared to your schedule, wakes up early in the morning to train, and takes a long time to get dressed: these are all things that you only come to know when you're living together and that you need to know how to accept. If your partner's habits start to bother you, there's only one strategy: be patient and love him as he is, without forcing him to change anything. Then, don't worry he will surely think the same about you too.

Tip 7: carve out some time just for yourself

Creating freedom in your relationship is a vital step in ensuring the longevity of your cohabitation. Moving in together is a step that leads to spending much more time with your partner. If we also start to neglect the various hobbies, going out with friends, and all the other habits we usually have when we live alone, then we risk living in symbiosis with our partner. All of this can be harmful both to the relationship itself and to all other relationships built outside the love story. For this, always remember to keep your spaces, i.e., your leisure activities, to continue going out with your friends, and not to miss those moments you spent without him.

Having hours to yourself will make you appreciate both your hobbies and your friendships and the presence of your partner when you come home who will be there waiting for you.

Never make your partner feel like you want to control him and take away his personal freedom. Instead, try to have the right mental flexibility to ensure that your partner has enough space to breathe. In this way, not only your partner, but also you, will have free moments from each other, but you also show him that you trust him and that you are sure of the solidity of your relationship. When your partner feels that he is truly free to be himself and to continue pursuing his passions even within cohabitation, then he will have no anxiety or doubts about spending the rest of his life with you.

Tip 8: avoid outside interference in your relationship decisions

Starting a cohabitation as a couple is a very delicate moment, especially if one allows one's parents, siblings, and relatives to invade the new married life with advice, appreciation, and various help. They often do this to voyeuristically control the couple. Letting them get in the way is a common mistake, but one that can have dangerous consequences.

Family intrusiveness in a newly cohabiting couple must be countered immediately: Boundaries must be clear from the outset by avoiding, for example, leaving the house keys with relatives.

The first rule that you will have to follow once you have started living together is We, first of all, which means that we give priority to our couple, our decisions, and our habits. Then, in the background, we put relatives and friends. This solidifies the couple and prevents problems of coexistence. This rule plans and establishes a total priority for the couple: everything else stays out, or at least stays in the background. Comments, controversies, stupid observations, free advice are filtered by this rule and, if they don't bring added value, they shouldn't even be taken into consideration.

Tip 9: Don't let your relationship become monotonous

One of the fundamental rules for making your coexistence work is to prevent the whole relationship from becoming routine. You will not have to take anything for granted, rather you will always have to be ready to make changes in different points of view. All relationships must always be nourished, with a new fire, so as not to fall into monotony.

What can probably make couples tired over time is a habit, believing they know each other, and not knowing how to speak. But relationships with people are not magically created: they must be taken care of day by day, with dedication and patience. Also, it's important to do things together. Slowly, day by day, you will lay very solid foundations, to become a couple who above all know how to renew and evolve together, making plans and even going outside the box.

Tip 10: Try to resolve issues by making compromises

All people have a different view of what is "normal" and when you decide to move in together your "normal" must match. Research and adopt a plan for each other's idiosyncrasies. It's not possible to have your partner always on your side and doing things exactly as you say, sometimes your partner may have his way or other times you may find a third mediation solution. When all these options aren't enough, learn to live with the fact that you don't have to do everything the same way. You can do it each in your own way.

Week 11. How to manage the decision-making aspects of the couple

All couples face situations in which they must make decisions. And whether or not they are important, they all require negotiation. It is perfectly normal to not agree on everything with your partner or to have differing opinions on how to make a choice. The decision-making process in the couple, in fact, does not consist only in taking a position for or against something; deciding together is proof of the strength and harmony of the relationship itself.

The opinion one has of oneself and the perception that one's opinion has value and weight has a great influence on the decision-making process in the couple. Confident people have all the resources to stand up for what they believe and influence the final decision. In other words, a person who believes in themselves has an active role in the couple's choices, while those who are insecure risk remaining in the shadow of their partner's decisions.

When it comes to deciding as a couple, a key aspect is given by the place that the other occupies in our idea of the future or life project. Decision-making is therefore based more on the future than on the present. The potential we see in the partner plays an extremely important role in his involvement in life projects such as: having children, getting married, or living together. The decision-making process in the couple is based more on mental anticipations than on the reality that one lives with the partner.

The decision-making process in the couple must be shared by both partners. The extent to which this happens will in fact be the indicator of a long-lasting and satisfying relationship.

When you choose to share your life with someone, you begin a journey in which you go from making decisions for yourself to doing it for two or, even better, for the well-being of the couple. It is a constant interlocking game in which compromises are promptly made, all the pros and cons of the situation are analyzed, and we try to imagine the consequences we will face both as individuals and, precisely, as a couple

On the other hand, it is equally necessary to strive to limit the external influences that can interfere with the couple's decision-making process. Prioritize what you and your partner feel, leaving the desire to please others in the background.

Being able to make important decisions together is one of the most difficult challenges but at the same time, it also represents a way to test the couple's relationship. Through the ability to relate to each other and to progress hand in hand without ever imposing on the partner, one can in fact understand a lot about both one and the person next to one. At the same time, it is possible to understand one's own limits and the duo's resources and work on them together to improve day by day, making the relationship more and more stable.

Tip 1: improve your ability to meet each other

The first thing you need to face each decision together concerns the ability to meet each other. In fact, by both remaining in one's own positions, there is the risk of never reaching an agreement or of giving way to those who are able to motivate their opinions more strongly. When you are a couple, however, it is important that every decision is taken together and that, as such, it is lived. In this way, regardless of the outcome, you can always count on the cohesion and support of the other person. Meeting each other therefore means talking to each other with an open heart, being sincere and never trying to bully the other person. All rules can sometimes be difficult to respect but, if followed, can lead to a couple of harmonies capable of repaying every small sacrifice.

Try to develop more confidence in yourself

To make decisions that are right, it is important to be confident and to know what you want and never want to include in your life. This assumption applies when you are single and becomes even more important in a relationship with two. Only knowing what you really want will be able to explain and motivate a decision. At the same time, you will be able to understand what your limits are, which is essential in order not to accept compromises that you cannot bear and which over time could lead to hating your partner.

Tip 2: try to be more empathetic toward each other

Just as it is important to know how to understand yourself, it is essential to do the same with your partner. It takes a certain amount of empathy to do that. Being able to hear how the other person is doing will in fact be easier to manage a conversation and understand what is good to propose and what should be avoided. Loving someone also means caring about their happiness, and that means worrying about their feelings and possible reactions. In a couple where both act in this way, even the most difficult decisions will be taken in harmony, making the couple a valid support to rely on for the well-being of both.

Tip 3: always talk to make the right decision

An aspect necessary for the general well-being of the couple that is equally important in decision-making is the ability to dialogue. In fact, it will only be by opening up to each other and understanding each other perfectly that we will be able to understand together where we are in the relationship, what we dream about for the future and what steps to take to get what we want. When a good basis for dialogue is at the basis of the relationship, even choosing which compromises to make in order to meet can be easier. Just as it is to understand what is important for the couple and how far one can or must go for their well-being. This obviously works if the dialogue is combined with a basic sincerity without which the basis for everything to work would be lacking.

Tip 4: always try to remain a united couple, even when deciding

Only a united and well-structured couple will in fact be able to carry on the entire decision-making process without losing harmony. And he will do it without letting himself be influenced by external opinions because he is aware that what matters within the couple is only the well-being of both. An aspect that is too often underestimated and which instead can make the difference, sanctioning a couple truly capable of teaming up and growing together in a syntonic way. Suitable for bringing them together and hand in hand towards the realization of important projects for both and always managed so as not to miss the balance of the couple.

Tip 5: avoid perpetual indecision

Haste is a bad advisor, but also putting off a decision too long becomes detrimental and exhausting for the couple. Each choice must therefore be made calmly, carefully evaluating the pros and cons, but once we get to the point, everyone will have to take their own responsibilities. Much of the confusion and nervousness within the couple arises precisely from the difficulty in defining common horizons.

Tip 6: Always consider risk management

Some decisions may end up being wrong and seriously impacting your life, such as quitting your day job or starting a business together. I'm not saying doing it all the time is wrong, it could be your family's way to become billionaires. However, in case things don't go as planned, there should also be a hands-on outing for the pair to get things back on track. In this case, always evaluate the pros and cons together and decide, always together, what might be the best solution.

Tip 8: never make important decisions for others too

never bully others, and impose yourself by asserting your opinion. Within the couple, it is healthy and normal to want to confront each other and ask for help and advice from the other, but this help and advice must only come if requested and not in a forced or imposed way.

Tip 9: try to find a new balance

Without a doubt, the most important thing when you are grappling with an important decision to make together is to find a new balance in the couple, trying to understand how to organize your spaces and your life together.

Have you gone to live in two different cities? Then it is important to understand immediately how to manage the relationship and how to see each other. Has one of you changed jobs and hours? The first thing to do is manage the moments when you are both free and try to reorganize your days.

In short, there are no magic formulas to find a new balance between you and every situation has a different solution, but the fundamental thing is to understand how to move from now on and build a new routine together.

Tip 10: always try to reach the right compromise

Compromise, when a decision has to be made and the two do not agree on the path to take, becomes the perfect meeting point between the two partners.

Finding a compromise means reaching an agreement. And when this agreement allows you to live happily, it is certainly a right and conscious choice. Compromise can be considered a constructive element in the relationship when it brings about an improvement for both without causing damage to one of the elements of the couple.

Finding the right compromise, therefore, means establishing a meeting point that brings two opposing parties to an agreement.

Week 12. How to improve mutual trust

Love is needed, but it's not enough, so it's essential to build trust in a couple's relationship. The feelings that unite two people are obviously the starting point and destination of a couple, which however also needs other elements that also make it solid.

Trust, precisely, is one of these elements which, contrary to what one might think, is something that must be built and cultivated over time, just like love.

Trust is one of the most important aspects of a relationship and in relationships in general.

The truth is trust requires commitment. If you are seriously committed to your partner and intuitively feel that they are trustworthy and of integrity, then you may be able to trust him or her to some degree. However, saying that your partner will always be there with you no matter what is difficult. Only a few are lucky enough to have this kind of relationship. So, you can never say you have total trust in your partner, but you can try to reach a level of trust that gives a certain sense of security.

Creating or recreating trust, especially after an event in which it has been questioned, is quite complex. In that case it is important that the couple decides to face it by both placing themselves in a constructive way.

Trust is therefore feeling comfortable, and safe with another human being and is of paramount importance in a relationship. When relationships begin, it is necessary to deposit trust in the other's emotional bank account with courteous, kind, honest behavior and by keeping the commitments made.

The advice that follows will help you trust your partner more consciously. They will help you develop a mindset based more on trust than suspicious or mistrustful attitudes. Always remember that, unless you have concrete proof of your partner's betrayal, always try to take his word for granted. Going around asking for information or spying on all your partner's movements and obsessively behaving like a control freak will only ruin your relationship.

So, if you are suspicious for no real reason, but you only do it out of senseless jealousy, forget it and don't start a fight, rather follow the advice you will find below to increase your trust in your partner.

Before talking about the tips that will increase trust between you and your partner, always remember that one of the best and most important ways to be able to trust each other is knowing how to apologize. In your long journey together, there will be times when you will argue and very often you will forget the promises you made. In these cases, knowing how to apologize is crucial to keeping your relationship alive. It often happens that in the couple one of the two, if not both, for various reasons is unable to apologize for the mistakes made. Know that this is just blind pride and selfishness and will only lead to the breakup of the relationship. So learn to admit your faults, especially if you have made a mistake or if you are wrong during a stupid argument.

Tip 1: learn to be together

To build trust in a relationship, it's important that you know how to be together. First of all, it is essential that partners share a couple value system.

Loyalty, for example, is not an issue to be taken for granted. It is good to be able to clarify from the beginning the positions regarding infidelity and everything that surrounds this concept. Explaining and sharing what could hurt the other is an important element in establishing trust in the couple.

Write each of your three main values and then check, if is there agreement between them. Are you building your lives and expectations on the same values? Do you share those roots that will determine your choices throughout your lives? Even if your values don't quite align, it's good to get to know each other to better understand your partner's intuitive processes and how her judgments are formed.

Tip 2: try to always be there, especially in difficult times

It's easy to enjoy each other's company when everything is going well but building trust in a relationship means much more. That is, knowing how to stand by your partner in difficult times. Neither should fear that a bad mood, nervousness, or worry will drive the other away. On the contrary, it is precisely in those moments that good communication facilitates the building of trust

Tip 3: Express your thoughts and feelings freely

No person can read another person's mind, even if she is the one, they love most in the world. Therefore, it is important that both partners can freely express their thoughts, emotions, and concerns, both individual and those concerning the couple. This is an exercise that continues to be practiced: even people in long-standing relationships can have moments in which they cannot express themselves adequately and, consequently, feel misunderstood by their partner. To build trust in a relationship, however, it's important to always try to make an effort to communicate so you can team up with your partner.

Tip 4: Always try to be honest

Trust in a relationship goes hand in hand, not to say directly coincides, with mutual sincerity. One thing can be little white lies (for example, if you lie to prepare a surprise), but in general, it is better for a couple to always be honest with each other. Sincerity and loyalty (that is, fidelity) are fundamental components for building trust in a couple's relationship. Whoever makes the mistake should admit it and apologize. Partners who lie often and intentionally will never reenter trusting relationships.

Also, discussing and talking about your insecurities with your partner will help you create a more sincere and open communication channel. Rather than jump into arguments where you do and say things that may appear crazy to each other, try apologizing for your behavior and explaining that your reaction isn't a lack of trust in your partner, but rather due to your personal insecurity.

Tip 5: Always prefer to be clear and transparent

Building trust in a couple's relationship also means not being afraid to show yourself vulnerable. It may not be easy for one or both partners: if you're not used to talking about the most intimate things, you can't change your attitude suddenly. But you can start creating situations where you feel comfortable broaching a touchy subject again. This is also a way to establish a relationship of trust with your partner.

Tip 6: never judge the other

To build trust in a relationship, there must be no judgments or preconceptions. A team that works is solid and supports each other even when you don't quite agree. Sometimes even a criticism or even a well-intentioned comment can hurt the other person at a time when they are vulnerable. So, don't judge. Instead, ask questions to better understand your partner.

Tip 7: give each other the space you need

Trust can never be forced; it must always be cultivated over time. Giving your partner space for himself allows him to reflect and evolve. In addition, this way the other can realize how much he misses you and how much he appreciates your company. In other words, this gives the other person a chance to get closer to you, which is a great way to build connection and trust. The love and attention that are given freely are by far the most precious of all.

Tip 8: never take the other for granted

Commit to stopping every now and then, taking some time to focus on what you value most in your partner and what he gives or does for you. In our fast-paced world, it's often easy to notice what your partner doesn't do, what they could do better, and what they did wrong. Make sure you pay enough attention to what works between you or what your partner does well. And then, let him know. Gratitude is an excellent key to triggering a positive spiral of feelings of trust and admiration in the couple.

Tip 9: give importance to the little things

In close relationships, small attentions are defined which are small continuous deposits over time that allow the share of trust in the emotional current account to gradually increase.

These small actions can be implemented occasionally but at the right time and for this very reason the other feels relieved, recognized, and helped. Other times, however, daily attention allows the other person to find gestures of affection every day.

The danger of daily deposits is that they can be taken for granted and only when they are missing can you really appreciate their importance.

Tip 10: Keep your commitments

Keeping commitments or promises is a primary deposit when this doesn't happen trust is consistently broken. Therefore, it is good not to make promises that cannot be kept, and it is good to clarify the situation when it is not possible to carry out a promise made due to unforeseen events.

People trust those who are consistent, so if a person is used to making promises that he doesn't keep, it will lead to an emotional account in the red and the crisis of a relationship.

Conclusion

Romantic relationships, to survive, as we have seen in this book, require hard work that must be done together with serenity and an open mind.

The benefits of resorting to the help of couples therapy described in this guide are endless. When you start to feel that you and your partner are going through a difficult time, this guide will help you improve your relationship and develop it further.

By the end of the 12-week course, you will have learned how to expand understanding, esteem, friendship, and closeness with your partner, also helping you to live a more fulfilling and happy relationship for both of you.

Remember, however, that if you want to achieve excellent results, both of you must be willing to learn to be more emotionally secure and well-disposed towards the other, that you must be more willing to open to dialogue rather than shutting down and sabotaging your life and that of your partner.

Finally, the willingness of both partners to assume their role in relationship issues and to make positive changes to maintain a healthy relationship is a prerequisite for the success of the therapy proposed in this guide.

I hope that the ideas that have been shared can help you strengthen relationships and the love bond with your partners. Which will help you deal with all the stormy situations that will arise in a positive way so that you can live a happy, lively, and lasting relationship.

Scan the QR CODE now to get the BONUS!

The 7 Pillars for Lasting Relationship

Made in United States
Orlando, FL
14 July 2023